A KEEPER OF WORDS

LEGEND: THE ARTHURIAN TAROT
by
Anna-Marie Ferguson

Awaken The Visionary Within Yourself

The Arthurian legend has fascinated and enchanted the Western world for centuries. It is our strongest and most compelling myth, embodying the romantic ideals of chivalry, bravery, and justice, the quest for goodness and truth, the tragedy and ecstasy of love, and the unconquerable spirit's victory over death.

Now this powerful myth has been joined seamlessly with the rich symbolism of the Tarot, to the enrichment of both. Context and direction are added to the deck by way of the Arthurian drama, and the traditional meanings of the cards are reinforced by the depiction of their compatible Arthurian guise. The blending of traditional Tarot symbolism with Pagan and Christian symbolism in the *Legend Tarot* has created a divinatory system which is infinitely rich and inspiring.

- Unites mythic elements from all four branches of the Arthurian legend: the Celtic legends, the early chroniclers, the medieval romances and the Quest for the Holy Grail

- Links every image in the traditional Tarot with its counterpart in Arthurian legend

- Explains the meaning of the archetypal Arthurian characters, events, and tales associated with each card

- Indicates the upright and reversed meanings for each card and how it relates to the legends

- Incorporates traditional Tarot symbolism with the legend's pre-Christian Pagan symbolism and the later Christian symbolism of the Grail Quest to enrich the cards' levels of meaning

Both the Tarot and Arthurian legend offer a fertile ground for psychic-spiritual development for, like the Tarot, myth communicates through symbols and archetypes, enabling us to grasp a higher knowledge of the great forces affecting our lives. The *Legend Tarot* is a captivating realm for anyone drawn to self-exploration via mythic journeys.

ABOUT THE AUTHOR

Anna-Marie Ferguson, a Scorpio, was born November 10, 1966, in the heart of the New Forest, Hampshire, England. When she was ten years old her family emigrated to rural Alberta, Canada. Anna returned to England in 1982 to undergo training in graphic design. She eventually returned to Alberta where she continued a career in design, devoting her spare time to developing her illustrating skills, ably assisted by her three cats.

Anna's fascination with Celtic legends and the Tarot began when she was a child in England. The atmosphere of the New Forest was steeped in history, and the faithful readings of the legends cultivated an appreciation of "the romantic" in Anna. Such formative influences have inspired Anna to keep this bygone age alive through her art.

TO WRITE TO THE AUTHOR

If you wish to contact the author or would like more information about this book, please write to the author in care of Llewellyn Worldwide, and we will forward your request. Both the author and the publisher appreciate hearing from you and learning of your enjoyment of this book and how it has helped you. Llewellyn Worldwide cannot guarantee that every letter written to the author can be answered, but all will be forwarded. Please write to:

Anna-Marie Ferguson
℅ Llewellyn Worldwide
P.O. Box 64383, Dept. K266–6, St. Paul, MN 55164-0383, U.S.A.

Please enclose a self-addressed, stamped envelope or $1.00 to cover costs.
If outside the U.S.A., enclose international postal reply coupon.

A KEEPER OF WORDS

Accompanying Book to

LEGEND:
THE ARTHURIAN TAROT

Written and illustrated by

Anna-Marie Ferguson

1998
Llewellyn Publications
St. Paul, Minnesota 55164-0383, U.S.A.

SECOND EDITION
Fourth Printing, 1998

Cover painting: Anna-Marie Ferguson
Cover design: Anna-Marie Ferguson and Anne Garrison
Illustrations: Anna-Marie Ferguson
Book design, layout, and editing: Jessica Thoreson

Library of Congress Cataloging-in-Publication Data
Ferguson, Anna-Marie, 1966-
     A keeper of words: accompanying book to Legend: the
     Arthurian tarot / written and illustrated by Anna-Marie
     Ferguson
        p.   cm.
     Includes bibliographical references and index.
     ISBN 1-56718-266-6 (book)
     ISBN 1-56718-267-4 (kit)
     1. Tarot. 2. Fortune telling by cards. 3. Divination.
     4. Arthurian romances—Miscellanea.   I. Ferguson,
     Anna-Marie, 1966-   Legend. II. Title.
     BF1879.T2F48   1995
     133.3'2424—dc20   95-1258
                                                       CIP

Publisher's note:
Llewellyn Worldwide does not participate in, endorse, or have any authority or responsibility concerning private business transactions between our authors and the public.
  All mail addressed to the author is forwarded but the publisher cannot, unless specifically instructed by the author, give out an address or phone number.

Printed in the United States of America

Llewellyn Publications
A Division of Llewellyn Worldwide, Ltd.
P.O. Box 64383, St. Paul, MN 55164-0383

To the old ghosts
who lend their stories

ACKNOWLEDGEMENTS

In creating *Legend: The Arthurian Tarot*, I am, quite naturally, beholden to the work of many gifted authors and historians. I would like to thank Count Nikolai Tolstoy for his inspiring work and the kind and encouraging words he and his family gave during the early stages of this project. Thanks are also due to Mr. Geoffrey Ashe, who took the time to clarify a point or two, and so help me on my way.

Legend would not have been possible if it were not for the support of Mr. and Mrs. Albert Gaught, and James Cameron, who bravely suffered my ceaseless chatter of the Tarot and all things Arthurian for what must have seemed an eternity. For their wisdom, guidance, and encouragement over the years, my heartfelt thanks to Peter Mason and Prudence Fitzalan Howard, who gave me my first Tarot deck on my eighteenth birthday. Credit is also due to Steven Williams, Paul Dickson, Ray Rue, and Phillip Toews, who patiently proofed my manuscript and scoured libraries and bookshops in search of any material that might help my cause.

Lastly, I acknowledge a great debt to the artist Allan Lee, whose graceful watercolours brought beauty and comfort to a young girl and inspired a fledgling artist. I am ever-grateful for his generous advice, kindness, and friendship.

CONTENTS

ONE: THE NATURE OF THE TAROT / 1

Introduction to the Tarot; the structure and divisions of the Tarot deck; the language of the Tarot; the common understanding and universal appeal of Tarot images; degrees of card reading; old misconceptions concerning the Tarot; cultural and religious aspects of the Tarot; the question of origin; a brief history of the Tarot

TWO: THE SPIRIT OF LEGEND: THE ARTHURIAN TAROT / 5

The value of myth; the compatibility of the Tarot and the Arthurian legend; the branches of Arthurian tradition; the symbolism of the deck; the blend of religions and their motifs; the use of the legend to add context to the Tarot; the tragic elements of myth; the titles of the cards and the suits; the symbolic significance of the maze design; the dragon face card, the layout board imagery, and the significance of the title "The Keeper of the High Word"

THREE: THE ARTHURIAN LEGEND / 9

Historical roots; the Dark Ages; political landscape; the Saxon threat; the coming of the Saxons; invading tribes; the struggle; the leaders; the Battle of Mount Badon; Arthur the historical warrior; early references to Arthur; achieving Celtic legendary status; brief account of the development of Arthurian literature; Celtic legend; the branches of Arthurian tradition, the histories of the chroniclers, the romances, and the Quest for the Holy Grail; transition to medieval ideal; change in religious tone; the legend's diversity

FOUR: CONSULTING THE TAROT / 13

How to begin; the importance of personal impressions of the cards; methods of card interpretation; the advantage of the Arthurian context; the significance of the Major and Minor Arcana; the nature of the suits, aces, and court cards; reversed interpretation; preparing for a reading; the significator card; dominant cards; the relationship between neighbouring cards; conflicting cards; the layout of the cards; the purpose and nature of a defined spread; Tarot reading as an analytic system; the Celtic Cross, sample reading; Astrological Spread; Horseshoe Spread

FIVE: NAVIGATING THE TAROT / 23

Moving beyond routine; the manner in which insights may appear; the importance of a comfortable atmosphere; rapport and receptivity; the abilities that distinguish a psychic reader; the borderland of the conscious and subconscious; focusing on hypnagogic dreams; heightening psychic awareness; overuse of the Tarot; rewards of patience

SIX: THE CARDS / 25

The interpretation and Arthurian context of the individual cards. The Major Arcana—the cards and the legends; the Minor Arcana—the cards and the legends: Spears, Swords, Cups, Shields

LIST OF CARDS

THE MAJOR ARCANA

The Minor Arcana

PREFACE

For centuries the heroic figure of King Arthur and the legends that surround him have inspired and entertained people of all ages. After nearly 1500 years the legend continues to provide a fertile ground for writers, poets, artists, etc., while presenting a complex and absorbing mystery for historians. Like many others, I was first introduced to the Arthurian world as a small child. Judging by my habit of assuming Arthurian names when playing childhood games, I believe it is safe to say the legend had left an impression. Admittedly at this young age I did not fully grasp the story; my confusion was made obvious by the fact that I often chose to be called Excalibur. Despite my limited understanding of the legend and its characters, the story had worked its magic, as I never forgot that powerful image of the sword rising from the lake. It was not until my early teens, when the school library purchased a copy of *King Arthur and his Knights*, that I became reacquainted with the tales. Over the following years I read on with renewed enthusiasm, eventually passing through the veil of romance to the Dark Ages. It was also during these formative years that I was introduced to the Tarot by way of a talented card reader who encouraged my interest. Over time, my small collection of Tarot and Arthurian books began to grow. Embarrassing though it is, I must admit that for years the two subjects stood side by side upon my shelf without my recognizing their compatibility. Nor did I read of the connection, which has been pointed out by others in the past, notably Jessie Weston in her book *Ritual to Romance*. The idea of combining the Tarot and the Arthurian legend eventually came to me while on a long, late night drive. No reasoning process led me to the conclusion, rather the idea just seemed to overtake me, leaving reason to follow. Naturally, I now count that long drive a blessing, as without it and its idle thoughts, I might have remained blind to what should have been obvious. By the end of my journey, I had connected all but one of the Major Arcana with their Arthurian counterparts. As one might well imagine, my excitement grew with each card. Fortunately, the inspiration and excitement I felt that night stayed with me throughout the creation of the deck.

Alongside my research, intuition has played an important role in the creation of *Legend*. This approach not only befits the nature of the Tarot, but given that the Arthurian research alone is the work of numerous lifetimes, I found intuition to be essential in navigating the Arthurian maze. The legend is far more than a grand tale for children, just as the Tarot is far more than a fortunetelling game. Both embody an age-old, collective wisdom which speaks on a deep, intuitive level.

The purpose of bridging the legend and the Tarot was to enhance the deck by providing a second avenue of approach. The frame of mythology serves to reinforce and clarify the traditional interpretations of the cards. Given the common thread that runs through the mythology and belief systems of different cultures, the coupling of the Arthurian legend and the Tarot seemed a very natural process. In creating this deck, I found the legend and the Tarot to be so compatible that I have come to believe that though their origins may be different, this is a marriage of old friends.

This book is only meant to provide a general introduction to the Arthurian world, and covers in abbreviated form only those aspects which relate to this particular Tarot deck. This is also true for the divinatory system of the Tarot, as both subjects could quite easily fill volumes—and lifetimes. There is a wealth of Arthurian literature available, far beyond the references listed in the back of this book. The list only includes those books which directly relate to the material contained in A *Keeper of Words*, and by no means includes all the books and authors to whom I am indebted. There are many authors and artists whose works have been a great source of inspiration, for which I am grateful. For practical reasons, I cannot note them all, but do encourage readers to further explore the mysterious Tarot and the Dark Ages—the realm of our once and future king.

ONE

THE NATURE
OF THE TAROT

The Tarot is a very old and sophisticated divinatory system. The wisdom and beauty of the mysterious cards have intrigued humanity throughout the ages. The Tarot embodies many profound and ancient teachings which pass far beyond their divinatory interpretations. For this reason, no one person ever truly comprehends all of its teachings, nor completes its study. The 78 cards of the Tarot are divided into two groups. The first 22 cards are called the trump cards or Major Arcana—Arcana meaning secrets. The Major Arcana begins with the Fool card numbered zero, and ends with the Universe or World card numbered twenty-one. The trump cards are rich in symbolism and can be considered the "Gate Keepers of Higher Knowledge." The remaining 56 cards, the Minor Arcana, are divided into four suits, each of which has fourteen cards: Ace through Ten, plus four court cards. The Minor Arcana tends to be less complicated than the Major, and helps to bring a card reading into focus.

The Tarot engages the student in a dialogue without words. Its language is symbolic; some of the paintings will seem to speak more to the reader than others. The same can be said of particular elements of the paintings, depending upon what is relevant to the reader at that time. Ultimately, each card will take on a higher personal significance as the individual becomes more familiar with the deck. The paintings embody the universal archetypes and mythological themes that are common to us all on a subconscious level. For example, the image of the cup or vessel speaks universally of fulfilment and nourishment. It is thought that this age-old symbolic language of the Tarot stimulates the subconscious and awakens the intuitive sense within the reader. Some archaic symbols are not quite so easily recognized or translated by the intellect; nevertheless, this does not diminish their ability to move us. Despite having lost direct contact with the significance of some of the ancient symbols, we are still instinctively drawn to and intuitively feel their essence. We do not, for example, fully understand the grand symbolism underlying the megalithic ring of Stonehenge or the Egyptian pyramids, yet many people are still attracted to and inspired by the ancient structures. It has been theorized that our universal appreciation, and occasional understanding of such things, may be due to our connections with what some philosophers have termed the *anima mundi*, or world-soul. The concept of the world-soul is closely related to that which the great psychologist Carl Jung termed the collective unconscious. The *anima mundi* is thought to contain the entire collective knowledge and memory, past, present, and future, of all living things. Thus, when the card reader moves beyond a mundane reading to a psychic reading, it is theorized that he or she has accessed that inherent part of the subconscious connected with the *anima mundi*.

A person does not have to believe in the prophetic ability of the Tarot to appreciate the cards, nor does one have to be a gifted psychic in order to read them. Naturally, those attuned to their intuitive sense will be able to take a reading a step further. With practice and patience, all can learn to read the cards and, hopefully, develop their psychic aware-ness in the process. The Tarot is a tool, and can be likened to a musical instrument. Most people can be taught the basics and can learn to play a tune. Those with the desire and discipline can become accomplished musicians. And then there are those with natural talent and keen dedi-cation who are capable of becoming masters of their art. There are card readers whose accuracy seems uncanny, so much so that they are often called psychic readers. Then there are card readers who claim no psychic ability, but nevertheless can provide insight through the traditional interpretations of the cards alone. Lastly, there are those, whom I would like to think are a minority, who misuse the Tarot by manipulating a reading to suit or further their own means. Not only is it disturbing to think that the Tarot would be used to take advantage of rather than to help people, but it also undermines the reputation of the Tarot in general. Unfortunately, there is no certain way to prevent those who are so inclined from misusing the Tarot. As with anything, there is the potential for abuse, whether it be a trusted relationship, a pitchfork, or a wagging tongue. If someone decides to read the Tarot for other people, he or she must be responsible and relay the information with a certain sensitivity, tempered with a common sense. Many positive developments can arise from a reading performed with good will. The Tarot can inspire, comfort, and encourage. This was my intent in painting these cards.

There has been the misconception that the Tarot was wicked or diabolical. Fortunately, with more and more people taking the time to study it, this somewhat silly notion is fading. As mentioned previously, the Tarot is like any other object; when used for its intended purpose it is a valuable tool. In and of itself the Tarot is not wicked. Most now recognize it for what it truly is—one of the many paths to greater spiritual understanding and self-awareness. Amidst the growing tolerance and inquisitive atmosphere, some churches have accepted the Tarot and encouraged its exploration as a method of enhancing spiritual awareness. The Tarot does not belong to any one religion, rather it is a mosaic of many. The traditional Tarot embodies the imagery and motifs of a wide range of cultures and belief systems, including Hindu, Christian, Islamic, and Pagan to name but a few.

The religious diversity of the Tarot has added to the difficulty of establishing its origins. There are a number of theories as to its source, but none are conclusive. Egypt and India have been popular contenders in the past, yet neither has been proved and both are often dismissed by historians. There is also uncertainty surrounding the age of the Tarot. The oldest surviving decks date from the mid-fifteenth century. Of these early cards, the hand-painted Italian decks known as the Visconti-Sforza Tarocchi are perhaps the best known. These rich and beautiful cards were the property of the Visconti and Visconti Sforza families. Toward the beginning of the sixteenth century, the Tarocchi made its way to France, and from there spread throughout Europe. Although it is commonly believed that the Gypsies introduced the Tarot and playing cards to Europe, historical evidence to support this idea is lacking. All early references to the Tarot connect it with the aristocracy, and playing cards were known to Europe many years before the arrival of the Gypsies toward the end of the Middle Ages. The Gypsies, however, may have been influential in promoting the divinatory use of the Tarot in later centuries. Given the expense of the early ornate cards, the Tarot was generally the property of wealthy noblemen of the day. With the arrival of the printing process, however, the cards became available to a greater percentage of the population.

For the 600 years or so that the Tarot has been in print, its imagery has remained largely intact. Each artist who has traveled this royal road has reincarnated the age-old arcana in his or her own artistic style, and one suspects has drawn on the *anima mundi,* or something like it, in the process. Over the centuries such renowned artists as Albrecht Dürer (reputedly), and more recently Salvador Dali have designed Tarot cards, as well as many talented and dedicated lesser-known artists. The poets William Butler Yeats and T. S. Eliot both held a fascination for the Tarot; Yeats even took the time to draw his own personal trump cards. Art historians, philosophers, authors, and laypeople alike have all been seduced by the elegance and mystery of the Tarot. With the renewed interest of recent years it seems likely that this ancient imagery will continue to flourish in the modern world.

TWO

THE SPIRIT OF LEGEND: THE ARTHURIAN TAROT

While remaining largely a traditional deck, *Legend* is set amidst the Arthurian world. Myth has the ability to dramatically express the universal patterns of life. Like the Tarot, myth communicates through symbols and archetypes and enables us to grasp, however fleetingly, a higher knowledge of the greater forces affecting life. Both myth and the Tarot are a creative expression of the internal experience of life and the forces of nature—in essence, an externalized drama of development. Mythology serves to bring context and structure to the experiences of life. The purpose of pairing the Tarot and the legend was to bring this added context and direction to the deck by way of the Arthurian drama. The traditional meanings of the cards are reinforced in *Legend* by the depiction of their compatible Arthurian tales. In gathering the 78 images for the cards, a number of Arthurian sources have been drawn upon, including the early chronicles, the medieval romances, and the Quest for the Holy Grail.

Celtic legend, beliefs, practices, folklore, and, when available, historical or Arthurian fact have also served in creating this deck. I say historical fact when available because there is relatively little known of this period in British history—aptly called the Dark Ages. The symbolism of the deck is a blend of traditional Tarot symbolism with the pre-Christian Pagan symbolism of the Celts and the Christian symbolism of the latter versions of the Grail Quest. This melding of the Pagan and Christian motifs reflects the atmosphere of the historical Dark Ages. This was a time of religious flux in which both belief systems existed side by side. The Arthurian legend itself mirrors this fusion as both Pagan and Christian imagery entwine within the saga. Despite the efforts of the Christian writers of later years to convert the legend, much of the early Celtic imagery prevailed.

This book only provides an abbreviated account of the archetypal Arthurian characters, deities, events, and tales associated with each card. In most instances the card focuses on one element of a longer story, and in some cases that particular story ends in tragedy. The later tragic ending is not meant to influence the interpretation of the card, rather the scene portrayed in the painting should remain the point of focus in a card reading. For example, the story connected with the Wheel of Fortune card tells of a powerful dream Arthur had the night before his last battle, in which he rides Fortuna's wheel. Fortuna favours him at first, setting him on top of her wheel and serving him fruit and wine. Eventually, she takes on a dark mood and spins her wheel, sending Arthur crashing down to the murky depths and the awaiting serpents. The painting depicts Arthur as he sits securely on top of the wheel, indicating a period of good fortune rather than the dreadful fate later experienced by Arthur.

Like any historical myth, there are frequent tragedies within the Arthurian realm. The Dark Ages were violent times and the stories often echo this precarious state. The Arthurian legend is a blend of history and myth, and as a myth it has to exhibit the essential, true-to-life experience of tragedy and despair; only then can it stage the powerful psychological drama and become a living myth.

The traditional titles of the Tarot cards appear above the painting, while the Arthurian title appears below, such as the Fool, which depicts Percivale. The only traditional titles changed are those of two suits. The more typical suit of Wands becomes Spears, and Pentacles becomes Shields. Though Spears and Shields were named so to accommodate the legend, it is not the first time they have appeared as suits. The fifteenth-century writings of Galcottus Martius mentions the suit of Spears, while the suit of Shields appears in Swiss tradition.

The design on the back of the cards is that of a maze known as "Julian's Bower"—a common name for mazes. This particular maze measures 40 feet in diameter and lies cut in the turf on a hillside in Lincolnshire. Before becoming a game of sorts, these ancient mazes were believed to have held a religious significance to the people who cut them. It is thought that they may have played a part in a kind of initiation ritual, and were symbolic of humanity's journey through life and our spiritual quest. There are a number of mazes throughout Britain, some in the form of earthworks and some carved into rock. Many of the designs carved in stone are considered to be the work of shepherds, and are traditionally thought to depict the fortifications of the City of Troy.

The dragon depicted on the face card of the *Legend Tarot* is the emblem of the Fellowship of the Round Table. Symbolically, the dragon represented the primal energies of the earth. Given that Arthur's father, Uther, took the sobriquet "Pendragon," meaning "Head Dragon" or "Foremost Leader," we may surmise that the title of "dragon" was used to refer to the rank of chieftain or overlord, and ultimately became a royal title.

The accompanying layout sheet follows the pattern of the Celtic Cross spread, the use of which shall be discussed later. The apple blossoms of the face card are repeated in the design of the layout board. The apple was considered Otherworldly and sacred to the Celts, and figures in many of their early legends. Boughs of apple travel the circle of the cross and the ladder, illustrating the seasons. The decorative interlacing that forms the circle is derived from a pattern on a Celtic brooch found in Ireland, which has been dated to approximately A.D. 700. Within the circle stands the Celtic World-Tree, which is equivalent to Yggdrasil of Norse mythology. Around the base of the Tree coils the Red Dragon of the Britons, which has remained the emblem of Wales through to the present day.

Lastly, it is worth noting the significance of the title of this book *A Keeper of Words*. In some versions of the legend we are told that Percivale is a descendant of the Grail Guardians. After achieving the Quest with his companions Galahad and Bors, Percivale fulfils his destiny in becoming the custodian of the sacred words, which we gather includes the mysterious "Grail question." In acquiring this charge, the Grail King dubs Percivale "The Keeper of Words" or "The Keeper of the High Word."

THREE

THE ARTHURIAN LEGEND

Though the origins of the Arthurian legend continue to be a topic of heated controversy, most would agree that underlying the fabled King Arthur of legend is a historical Dark Age figure. The Dark Ages is a period of European history from the fifth to the tenth centuries. Within this time frame we find the period known as Arthurian Britain, beginning with the year A.D. 400 following the Roman withdrawl from Britain, and concluding around A.D. 650. The Arthurian Age was a perilous time for the Britons. For many years they had contended with European raiders, but none had had such an impact nor been so alarming as the invading Saxons. Having overrun what is now Holland, the Saxons launched their ships and made their way to Britain. "Saxon" was the term conveniently used to refer to not only the Saxons, but the invading Jutes and Angles as well. Though the Saxons gained relatively little ground, their raids were fierce. The Britons not only had to contend with the Saxons, but also the encroaching Picts and Irish tribes, who the Romans called the Scots. Ultimately, Britain was surrounded by aggressors. The Saxons grew in numbers and daring. The Angles allied themselves with the Picts, and by his rash decisions King Vortigern of the Britons recklessly aided the

Saxon cause and made his country grieve. Eventually, Britain's defenses collapsed under the combined stress of the invading nations, and terror was unleashed and spread throughout the land. It was the historical leader Ambrosius Aurelianus (Aurelius Ambrosius, in legend) who rallied the Britons and led them against the invaders, regaining a substantial amount of the lands that had been lost.

The Britons continued to fight the tenacious Saxons for a period of approximately 40 years. During this time there were victories and defeats for both forces. It was not until the famous Battle of Mount Badon before a clear victor emerged. It is here, with the fighting men of Mount Badon, that we find the historical Arthur—not as king, but as an exemplary military leader who fought alongside the Kings of Britain. It is here, with the triumph over the Saxons, that Arthur and his warband secure their heroic standing which would come to inspire a legend.

The northern bard Aneirin alluded to the supreme battle skills of Arthur in the early seventh-century poem *Gododdin*. While praising the skill of a later hero in a later battle, the author concedes that the hero achieved great feats, "though he was not Arthur." We can see from the *Gododdin* that within a relatively short time Arthur's prowess became legendary.

Historia Brittonum ("History of the Britons"), from the early ninth century, contains the first mention of Arthur in a historical sense. Though the identity of the author remains uncertain, the work is generally attributed to the monk Nennius. The *Historia* names Arthur as the leader of the British forces at Mount Badon and gives a list of his eleven previous battles. Thought to have been compiled in the early tenth century, the *Annales Cambriae* makes two references to Arthur. The first is in connection with Mount Badon, and the second refers to the battle of Camlann, known in legend as the last battle, "in which Arthur and Medrawt fell."

Over 600 years, many stories accumulated around Arthur and his warband. The first to bring form to this bemusing blend of mythology and history was Geoffrey of Monmouth, in his quasi-historical *Historia Regum Britanniae* ("History of the Kings of Britain"). Geoffrey wrote his *Historia* in the early twelfth century, but maintained that he had only copied it from a very ancient book in the British language. With Geoffrey's work, the previously fragmented Arthurian stories became coherent.

Near the same time, the Welsh *Mabinogion* was compiled, the characters of which have appeared in Arthurian tradition. The collection of tales that makes up the *Mabinogion* are drawn from the rich Celtic mythological tradition. Due to the language, some of the tales are believed to predate the eleventh century. The twelfth century held another important development in the shaping of the legend, which lies in the arrival of romance with the poems of Chrétien de Troyes. Many poets drew on the *Matter of Britain* for inspiration, but it is with this French poet that we have the beginning of the branch of Arthurian tradition known as the romances.

With the poems of Chrétien de Troyes we gain the first romance concerning the Grail Quest. It is generally agreed that Chrétien de Troyes had previous knowledge of the earlier Celtic tales and used these in his work. Literature concerning the Quest for the Holy Grail has become a field of study in itself. With the romances, Arthur the Dark Age warrior and his warband are transformed into the medieval ideal. The rough band of warriors become the courteous Knights of the Round Table. Arthur becomes the fatherly king who resides, not in a hillfort, but in the fantastic Camelot. His role is diminished to presiding over the Fellowship and quietly attending to affairs of state. In the romances, the knights take centre stage, going to and fro on a bewildering array of adventures. There is also a change in the religious tone of the legend during the medieval period, as Christian themes and ideals began to replace or overlay the earlier Celtic elements.

In the fifteenth century, Sir Thomas Malory undertook the awe-inspiring task of compiling and trying to reconcile the work of the early chroniclers, the romances, and the Quest for the Holy Grail in his *Le Morte d'Arthur*. Undoubtedly, Malory had a great passion for the subject, for he left us with a wonderfully written, and for the most part, coherent account of the Arthurian saga.

A number of sources have been used in creating *Legend*, including those discussed here, but generally the source of the stories incorporated into the Tarot ends here in the fifteenth century with Malory's *Le Morte d'Arthur*, which together with Geoffrey of Monmouth's *History of the Kings of Britain*, forms the foundation of *Legend: The Arthurian Tarot*.

In exploring *Legend*, one may find versions of the tales that differ from those familiar to the reader. The Arthurian legend is a living legend, in that it has been retold and reshaped countless times over the centuries. The storytellers of each age have continually developed the tales, drawing on, modifying, and highlighting those aspects which reflect the prevailing views of their times. As a natural consequence of its popularity and diversity, one will find that discrepancies and inconsistencies occasionally appear. Those who further investigate the Arthurian realm (as I would certainly encourage) may find that the name of the hero of a particular adventure may change, as well as the details of his or her experience. The nature of the character may also change. Morgan le Fay, for example, may be portrayed as a revered priestess or a menacing witch, depending on the author. In knowing this, the conflicting accounts are apt to be less confusing and can be seen as an enriching quality of a legend that has known 1500 years of life.

FOUR

CONSULTING THE TAROT

The first step in learning to read the Tarot is to become familiar with the imagery of the cards. Slowly go through the deck and contemplate each card. Initially, the 78 cards can seem overwhelming and nearly impossible to absorb in one sitting, but if one takes some quiet time over a few days the images will begin to settle in the mind. At this stage, it is worth noting your own personal impression and interpretation of the cards before learning the traditional meanings. Not only is it interesting to see how the two compare, but in writing out the impressions, one begins to personalize the deck. These early, pure impressions can bring further insight, and may be added to the traditional interpretations.

Once one is familiar with the paintings, learning their significance becomes much easier. Some people choose to memorize the meanings of the cards, starting with the Fool and working their way through the deck. Others investigate their favourite cards first, and concentrate on the paintings that appeal to them at the time. The method used really depends on what suits the individual, but what should be stressed is that the traditional interpretations are only meant to provide a foundation and general direction upon which the reader can expand, as by themselves the traditional interpretations can make for a rather stiff card reading. By the same token, if one reads according to personal interpretations, the reading is again restricted to the reader's knowledge and experience of life. It would seem that the greatest success comes from a combination of both methods. The traditional meanings act as a starting point for further interpretation, and can help to prevent the reader from projecting his or her wishes or fears into the reading. Given that each card can have more than one meaning, intuitive thinking ought to serve as a guide and balance the two methods of interpretation. During the early stages, one often depends mainly on the meanings listed in the book. This is to be expected, but with time and practice, one will find less and less need for it. There is a great advantage to be gained in reading the Arthurian aspect associated with each card, as the stories and characters tend to be far more memorable than the card interpretations alone. The context they provide can help a great deal in understanding and remembering the significance of each card. Those who are familiar with numerology and astrology will have an added means of approaching the cards. The number of the card also carries a significance. For example, the number one would refer to beginnings, while ten would point to completion, climax, turning point, etc. The ruling planet or zodiac sign associated with each card of the Major Arcana are listed in this book, and again add insight to the nature of the card.

To quickly review the grouping of the cards, the first 22 cards are the Major Arcana, or trump cards. The remaining 56 are divided into four equal suits which make up the Minor Arcana. The trump cards signify a powerful influence, and what some call cosmic influences in your life. The Major Arcana cards tend to be fatalistic and reflect important stages of development. The Minor Arcana tend to represent aspects of one's life that are within the individual's control. The four suits—Spears, Swords, Cups, and Shields—symbolize different qualities and facets of life which are, respectively, ideas and the intuitive intellect; action and logic; emotions and creativity; material well-being, security, and values. Each suit runs Ace through Ten; the Ace represents the purest form of the energy symbolized by the suit. These cards are followed by four court cards—the Page, Knight, Queen, and King. *Legend* substitutes a totem animal for the young man who generally represents the Page in traditional Tarot decks.

The court cards can symbolize the querent's state of being or aspiration, as well as other individuals who influence the situation. The court cards are not limited to gender, as they can reflect the feminine and masculine characteristics inherent in all of us.

Knowing that many card interpreters use reversed cards in their Tarot readings, the reversed meanings of the cards have been included in this book. However, if one chooses to use reverses, it should be kept in mind that if a card lands in a reversed position, it generally indicates that the particular energy of the card is being stifled or blocked, rather than indicating disaster. Given the diversity and extensive design of the Tarot which encompasses and balances both the obstacles and rewards of life, I personally feel that reverses needlessly add to confusion and can make for an unnecessarily disjointed reading.

Having become accustomed to the cards and their meanings, the next step is to learn the traditional practices in preparing for a reading and the card layout patterns, called spreads. Before a reading begins, some readers choose one card from the deck that they think best describes the person for whom they are reading. If they do not know the person well, they may ask the querent to choose for him or herself. This card is called the significator, and is believed to help focus the reading. This lone card is then set aside while the remaining cards are shuffled by the reader. When you shuffle the cards, make an effort to clear the mind of any preconceived ideas of what the reading may present. It is important that you be relaxed and comfortable in order to become receptive to the intuitive insights that will hopefully arise during the reading. It is equally important that the querent be relaxed so that he or she may concentrate on the issues he or she wishes to explore. Once the cards are shuffled they are then cut, usually by the querent. Beyond this, the querent has very little contact with the cards, as it is generally thought that the less people touch them, the better. This tradition is meant to preserve the personal feel of the deck. Having cut the cards, the reader then lays them out, face up, in the order and pattern of the chosen spread. Before one begins to interpret the individual cards, scan the entire layout to see if you can recognize the semblance of a story being told by the positioning of the cards. At this stage it is also a good idea to explain and reassure the querent about the significance of any of the rather grim cards that may appear in the layout. For those not familiar with the meaning, the sight of the Hanged Man, for instance, can be somewhat alarming. During this initial overview of the spread, make sure to take into account the dominant cards in the layout. For example, if the Major Arcana are prevalent, one knows this is a period of important growth in which great change is possible. Whereas, if the suit of Shields make up the majority, then the reading is more apt to reflect material concerns. This quick overview can help set the tone of the reading. The third thing to note is the relationship between neighbouring cards, as this can influence and clarify the meaning of a card. A case in point would be the effect of the Five of Shields on the Nine of Swords. (I apologize for the gloomy choice of cards, but they do illustrate rather well the subtle ways in which the cards can modify one another.) The Nine of Swords (The Lily Maid) can indicate a lingering and debilitating feeling of depression, which stems from something other than the person's current environment. The Lily Maid grieves despite her pleasant surroundings. Now, if the Five of Shields (The Wasteland) were to be her neighbour, it would cancel out the "pleasant surroundings" of the Lily Maid and point to an inhospitable and unstable environment, causing worry and adding to the stress. In this case, one quality is suppressed and another enhanced, but often the cards can reinforce each other. Occasionally, one may come across two cards that contradict one another. Here, one must pay attention to the surrounding cards further afield to bring context, as well as give particular attention to the aspects of the paintings which speak loudest during the reading, as they provide important clues.

There are a variety of spreads from which one can choose; some are short and concise, while others require a large number of cards and can become quite involved. Each position in a spread designates a particular aspect or influence in one's life. As with the interpretations of the cards, the definition of the positions may vary slightly between card readers. Having become accustomed to the dynamics embodied in a traditional card spread, one may want to develop a personal layout—creative use of the Tarot is encouraged.

Perhaps the oldest and most widely used layout is the Celtic Cross. Its popularity is a result of its ability to provide insights into a number of areas in one's life, while relating a sense of story and time. The second layout provided here is the Astrological Spread. It follows the pattern of an astrological chart, and can be interpreted in the same way—the first house, Aries, reflects the personality and behaviour of the querent; the second house, Taurus, indicates financial matters and possessions, etc. The Astrological Spread can also be used for a general forecast of the coming twelve months. The third layout is known as the Horseshoe

Spread and is a handy, quick little spread, designed for questioning a specific issue.

The advantage of defined traditional spreads, like the three discussed, is their ability to bring structure and ground ideas and concerns that would otherwise continue to swim in one's mind. By externalizing the situation and focusing on the cards, the reader and the querent can view the matter and the contributing influences in an objective manner. Even if the future remains elusive, the overview and the exercise of exploring all aspects and influences in one's life can help the querent by instilling a sense of order, direction, and control. The benefits of the Tarot as an analytical system may outweigh its oracular use, as it allows the querent to distance him or herself from a situation, make a direct evaluation, and take charge of his or her own destiny. As we all know, we can, at times, feel so overwhelmed that we cannot see the woods for the trees. In cases like these, whether one believes in the prophetic quality or not, the system of the Tarot and the structure it provides can be a valuable analytic tool.

THE CELTIC CROSS

Place the significator in the centre of the cross, then deal out ten cards, face up, in the order indicated by the diagram on the following page.

The first six cards which form the cross refer to the querent's present circumstances, while the four which form the ladder refer to the direction of the future, if the querent continues on the present path (in most cases one can affect the outcome reflected by the cards with a conscious effort).

INTERPRETATION OF CARD POSITIONS

Position 1: Indicates the querent in relationship to the present situation.

Position 2: Represents the positive forces or assets in the querent's favour. If this card should happen to be a negative card, it indicates the nature of an obstacle that is hindering progress. (The card in this position is always interpreted in its upright manner.)

Position 3: Can be viewed as a message from the "higher self." It can also reflect the querent's potential and aspirations.

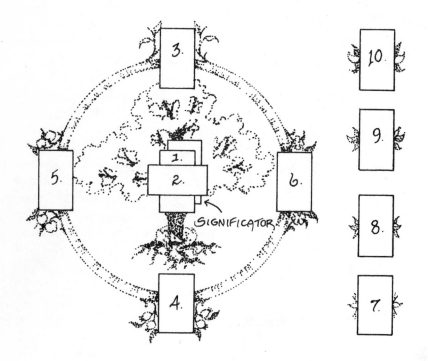

Position 4: Represents the preoccupation of the subconscious which filters into waking life, affecting moods and outlook. This is the underlying theme of dreams and the emotional undercurrent in the querent's life.

Position 5: Represents past events and influences that colour and give rise to the current situation.

Position 6: Represents the state of the querent's relationships with others.

Position 7: Indicates the querent's psychological state and attitudes which can greatly affect the outcome of the matter.

Position 8: Represents the querent's environment and unseen forces influencing the situation.

Position 9: Indicates the hopes and fears of the querent.

Position 10: Indicates the outcome of the matter.

SAMPLE READING USING THE CELTIC CROSS

In this sample reading, the cards fall as follows:

Position 1: King of Swords

Position 2: Seven of Swords

Position 3: Six of Spears

Position 4: Ace of Spears

Position 5: Page of Spears

Position 6: Six of Swords

Position 7: Queen of Spears

Position 8: Ace of Swords

Position 9: The Fool

Position 10: Knight of Shields

When scanning all the cards we see that the majority are Spears and Swords. Adding further impact to the significance of the suits is that the Ace of both Spears and Swords appears. This leads to the conclusion that the reading concerns putting ideas into action. We know from the presence of Spears that the querent has an idea, or perhaps several related ideas and plans, and so the King of Swords in position number one is a welcome sight, for he represents determination, ambition, and a decisive personality, giving him the qualities needed to persevere with the idea and put it into play. The second card, Seven of Swords, reflects his ability to inspire others, rally support, and launch a project, or as in the painting, initiate a quest. The third card, Six of Spears, encourages perseverance, and indicates that focus can bring victory, respect from others, celebrations, and relief. The fourth card doubles its power, as the Ace of Spears represents the intuitive intellect, which is related to the subconscious, and position number four represents the subconscious. Here we have the subconscious working in unison with the conscious toward a truly inspired idea. One would surmise that it originated here in the subconscious, and was carried by the intuitive sense of Spears and, fortunately, was recognized by the intellect, symbolized by Swords. The fifth card indicates enthusiastic support from others in the recent past. Taking into account the following card, the Page of Spears could be read as having received an invitation to travel to present the idea. At this point the gentleman for whom the reading is being performed confirms that he does have an idea and had an enthusiastic response, but he has yet to present it to would-be investors. In looking at the cards, you would think the opportunity is approaching fast; it should be nearly on top of the querent, as the sixth card is the Six of Swords—travel, adventure, a mission which involves meeting new people of a distant place. There is progress ahead. Knowing now the nature of the mission, the seventh card, the Queen of Shields, could represent an investor. On the other hand, if it were to be interpreted according to its position, it would represent the tactful, thorough, and convincing presentation of the idea. The eighth card, the Ace of Swords, is another welcomed sight, as it can represent getting results and a tremendous amount of energy at the querent's disposal. The ninth card, the Fool, one's hopes and fears, is quite straightforward—hoping one's expectations are realistic and fearing disillusionment, and perhaps worrying about lack of experience. The tenth card, the Knight of Shields, while not truly conclusive, does end the reading on a positive note, with steadfast progress; quite possibly the financing has come through and the work involved in realizing the idea has begun. Timing aside, the reading indicates a promising future for this gentleman and his inspired idea. This particular line up of cards could be interpreted in numerous ways, with the details varying somewhat, but "acting on ideas" remains the essence of the reading.

THE ASTROLOGICAL SPREAD

Place the significator in the centre, then deal twelve cards counterclockwise from position number one to form the circle.

Position 1: Aries—reflects the querent's personality, attitudes, and how he or she interacts within the world.

Position 2: Taurus—reflects financial matters and material possessions.

Position 3: Gemini—relates to education, communications, siblings, and travel.

Position 4: Cancer—reflects home, family, roots, childhood, and fatherly influences.

Position 5: Leo—represents creativity, romance, leisurely pleasures, and relationships with children.

Position 6: Virgo—reflects work ethics, health, responsibilities, and helping others.

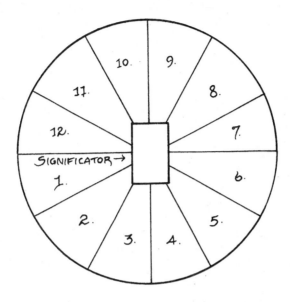

Position 7: Libra—reflects marriage, close partnerships, alliances, and working relationships.

Position 8: Scorpio—represents hidden influences, life cycles, sexuality, and psychic abilities.

Position 9: Sagittarius—reflects philosophies, religion, law, long-distance travel, and foreign cultures.

Position 10: Capricorn—represents career, ambitions, achievements, public status, and self-esteem.

Position 11: Aquarius—reflects social life, acquaintances, and hopes and wishes.

Position 12: Pisces—represents the subconscious, strengths and weaknesses, and restrictions with which one is faced.

The Astrological Spread may also be used for a general twelve-month forecast.

THE HORSESHOE SPREAD

Position 1: Past conditions.

Position 2: Querent's present situation.

Position 3: Future outlook.

Position 4: Best approach to the situation.

Position 5: The attitudes of others surrounding the querent.

Position 6: Challenges to be faced.

Position 7: The final outcome.

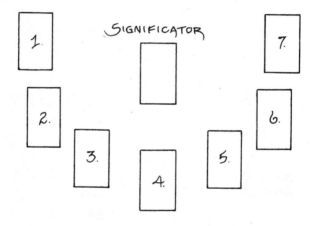

FIVE

NAVIGATING
THE TAROT

Occasionally, a Tarot reading may move beyond the framework of traditional card interpretation and become a psychic reading. Realistically one cannot expect every reading to be a psychic reading; more often than not a reading will involve card interpretation and only vague intuitive feelings, which, while they may persist, tend to remain on the tip of one's tongue. Whether a reading brings psychic insights depends on a number of things. A comfortable, private atmosphere is of utmost importance. Another important factor, over which we admittedly have little control, is whether there is a rapport between the reader and the querent. This connection can make all the difference as to whether the reader senses currents and developments or dead air.

The rate of psychic readings, as compared with the number of more mundane readings, depends largely on the reader's ability to recognize and translate the sensations, impressions, and images roused by the suggestive paintings of the Tarot. When the reader is calm and relaxed he or she becomes more receptive, and the reading is more likely to take on an intuitive or psychic edge. The reader may see flashes of images or experience spontaneous ideas, words, impressions, and sensations that can be likened to the sensation of *déjà vu*. Since all people dream, and most have experienced *déjà vu* or some sort of related sensation, such as a strong intuitive impression or instinct, it would stand to reason that we are all capable of connecting with the intuitive or psychic sense thought to lie in the domain of the subconscious.

The difficulty is in catching the fleeting images and impressions. One exercise that can help in becoming accustomed to this borderland between the conscious and subconscious is to pay close attention to dreams. Not so much the epic dreams, but rather the little dreamlets, called hypnagogic dreams. These dreamlets are common at the onset of sleep, when one is neither truly awake nor asleep. This seems to be a time when the rising subconscious and setting conscious eclipse each other, for lack of a better word. This brief period gives rise to some truly bizarre images and voices. Some seem to make no sense at all, while others tend to be highly symbolic, and some, I dare say, are precognitive, or so I have found in my own experience. For this reason it is worth keeping a dream diary. Trying to focus on these dreamlets or flashes is easier said than done. If the conscious mind takes the foreground, "the show is over"—yet when the subconscious overtakes, as it eventually does, the audience is asleep. This balancing act is difficult to maintain for any length of time, but with practice, one can train the conscious to catch a few of the elusive images. Working with the Tarot should help in heightening one's psychic awareness, but exercises such as the one above, along with meditation or any creative pastime, will further attune one's psychic sense. It should be kept in mind that overuse of the Tarot can dampen one's abilities as well as lead to an unhealthy dependency upon the cards. Above all, remember to be patient as the Tarot is a complex system that one cannot expect to learn overnight, and even accomplished readers have off days when nothing seems to make sense.

The rich, symbolic world of the Tarot holds infinite possibilities and many rewards for those willing to study it, whether they happen to be psychic or not. It was the mysterious artwork of the Tarot and not its prophetic application that drew my initial attention, and I must say, I began my journey through the Tarot with what could be termed as a healthy scepticism in this regard. Years have passed, and still I cannot intellectually fathom the inner working of the Tarot, nor can I deny the uncanny insights these age-old cards can provide. There is only one matter of which I am certain—the wise and enchanted world of the Tarot has my respect.

SIX

THE CARDS

The interpretation and Arthurian context
of the individual cards

THE MAJOR ARCANA

0. THE FOOL
Ruled by Uranus

PERCIVALE

MEANING

The beginning of adventure; establishing a path. The enthusiasm which accompanies the onset of a new project or idea. The dawn of new experiences, the broadening of horizons, and the envisioning of goals and ambitions.

Unaware of the pitfalls, one embraces the future with great optimism. Depending on the surrounding cards, this innocence and undaunted manner may serve one well, inspiring others with one's infectious energy. In such a state of mind one is free to enjoy life and indulge in wonderful, if occasionally unrealistic, imaginings of the future.

REVERSED

Excessive, irrational behaviour. The disregard of or inability to recognize worthwhile opportunities. The delay of growth as a result of insecurity; the lack of conviction that leads to aimless wandering without fulfilment. Ignoring the heart's desires in favour of an easier route.

DESCRIPTION AND SYMBOLISM

Percivale looks to his future—Camelot. The clouds part and the sun shines, revealing the castle in all her splendour. Washed clean by the rain, she shows her best face to the newcomer. For Percivale, this represents an inviting opportunity, the fairy-tale scene encouraging his hopes and ambitions. The emblem of the Knights of the Round Table hangs over the gatehouse, representing a realistic goal, achievable with discipline. The scene symbolizes a return to the sense of wonder, optimism, and faith commonly felt in childhood. The dog expresses this exuberance and playful nature, reflecting Percivale's positive outlook and bright hopes for the future. Everything about the card is fresh and new. The green of the trees symbolizes fertility and possibilities; the blue butterfly, beauty and freedom; the clear river, purity and good will.

Percivale gazes at the emblem of the Round Table. This expresses his infatuation with the goal while neglecting the path. He seems oblivious to the fact that he stands on a ledge. Likewise, he does not notice the squires who tend the horses. This warns that one must pay attention to details, the sacrifices, and struggles that exist on the path to any goal. At this point Percivale is unaware that before becoming a knight he must first be a squire. The adventure begins ...

PERCIVALE

ercivale (Parsi-fal = "Pure Fool") spent his childhood in a remote part of Wales. In being so far from the court his mother had hoped to shield him from the heroic songs and tales that would encourage him to take up a career in arms. Despite all her efforts, however, Percivale encountered this foreign world when one afternoon he happened across some of Arthur's knights passing through the forest. Having never seen a knight before, Percivale was dazzled by the sight and thought them to be angels. Much to his mother's dismay, Percivale was determined to follow them to Camelot and become a Knight of the Round Table. It broke her heart to think of the dangerous and violent life Percivale had chosen, but in realizing nothing would dissuade her innocent and inquisitive son, she saw him off with the gift of a new homespun tunic and some words of advice. (See Three of Shields.) On arriving in Camelot, Percivale promptly asked to be made a knight. All laughed at his ignorance, but Arthur kindly explained that he would have to earn the title by rising through the ranks, beginning as kitchen knave. The young Percivale caused chaos wherever he went, but even though he tried people's patience most looked upon him with affection.

Percivale matured and eventually received his knighthood. In the early days of his career he happened upon a maimed man fishing from a boat. Unknown to Percivale, this man was the Fisher King, who offered the young knight lodgings in his nearby castle. Although grateful for the invitation, Percivale was surprised and puzzled—he had been told there were no castles for many miles. While in the Grail Castle, Percivale was witness to the mysterious procession of the Grail. The young lodger remained silent as it passed before him and into an adjoining chamber. It was a strange and wonderful sight, like nothing he had ever seen. Thinking himself polite, Percivale restrained himself from asking any questions concerning the Grail. This was a very unfortunate circumstance, for had he asked, thereby showing interest and concern, both the Fisher King and his wasting lands would have been healed. Having failed this test, Percivale awoke the next morning to find himself alone in the mysterious castle. Quite baffled, Percivale mounted his horse and left the castle. As he neared the end of the drawbridge, however, it began to close, seemingly of its own accord. Horse and rider were forced to jump to reach the bank. Percivale would later realize his grave mistake in failing to ask the question and would spend many years trying to find the Otherworldly Castle of the Grail.

Percivale eventually became one of Arthur's greatest knights. Percivale, Galahad, and Bors made up what is known as the Three Elect—the three who would achieve the Holy Grail. On his second visit to the castle, Percivale and his companions were successful. Galahad healed the wounded king, lifting the curse over the land (in earlier accounts Percivale is the hero, as Galahad is a later literary addition to the story). Having looked deep into the mystery of the Grail, Galahad no longer wished to live and died amidst great beauty. The Grail King instructed Bors to carry the news to the world, dubbing him "The Messenger." He then appointed Percivale his replacement as Grail Guardian, dubbing him "The Keeper of the High Word."

1. THE MAGICIAN
RULED BY MERCURY

MERLIN

MEANING

Skill and wisdom. The noble use of one's talents. A state of harmony with one's environment. Possession of the power of influence. A wise counsellor. Sensitivity to unseen powers. Independent thought.

Awareness of one's role in the community. Showmanship and originality win respect and inspire others to follow. The self-confidence needed to take risks and direct one's life. The strength of will and self-discipline needed to complete a task or training. Diplomacy in business transactions that brings positive results. Grace under pressure.

REVERSED

Deception. A drain of energy. Loss of direction. Not seeing the forest for the trees. Unbalanced thinking. An inability to rise above or see beyond the immediate situation. Defensive behaviour. Negative use of power. A manipulating trickster.

DESCRIPTION AND SYMBOLISM

Merlin retreats to the isolation of his mountain cave. Surrounded by nature he is able to centre himself and connect with the forces that work through him. This solitary existence allows him to hear the words of the winds and learn of things yet to come.

Merlin is the guardian of the Sacred Spring which flows in the foreground, representing the wise and honourable use of precious resources.

A wolf was said to have kept company with Merlin. This familiar symbolizes the magician's sensitivity to the forces of the wild. His powers come from understanding their nature rather than from their domination. It is a relationship not of fear, but of mutual respect.

Foxgloves grow alongside the stream. Having long been associated with the faery, they are a reminder that Merlin neither dwells nor works alone. He is surrounded, inspired, and assisted by the unseen spirits of the wood, the dryads. The plant itself is extremely poisonous—a bringer of death—and yet when refined it is a powerful cardiac medicine—a giver of life. This illustrates the crucial preparation, training, and knowledge needed if one is to advise or lead others. It also serves as a warning against overconfidence, as there are always dangers present when engaging powers of a dual nature.

Merlin's rich blue cloak represents his honoured standing in the world of men, while the feathers are a symbol of the shaman's spiritual flight and metamorphosis.

MERLIN

erlin is one of the most famous and fascinating Arthurian characters. Though it is likely that Merlin the sage did exist, the embroidered Merlin of legend is most probably a composite of several historical figures and Celtic gods.

Merlin was born a fatherless child of a virgin, which when coupled with his uncanny gifts, led others to believe that his was an unnatural birth. This suspicion surrounding his origin meant that although Merlin would come to be respected, he was also feared. On occasion, Merlin would use this fear to his advantage. As chief druid, Merlin had a close relationship with the Damsels of the Lake. He was a prophet, poet, engineer, and counsellor to the High Kings. With an eye always on the future of Britain, Merlin often helped shape future events, and as the following tale demonstrates, he played a crucial role in the birth and ascendency of Arthur.

The beautiful Igraine first met the newly crowned High King Uther when accompanying her husband, the Duke of Cornwall, on a visit to London. Uther's attraction to her was immediate and before long the king could think of nothing else. Sensing the brewing trouble, the duke abruptly left London, taking Igraine back to Cornwall and securing her within the walls of Tintagel. Uther followed under the pretence that the defiant duke intended to undermine his reign. Uther's men clashed with the duke's forces, but still the cliffs of Tintagel and the sea kept Igraine beyond Uther's reach. Driven by frustration, Uther turned to Merlin for help.

Upon hearing the story, Merlin became annoyed with the king for having risked civil war over his love for Igraine. After careful thought, however, Merlin agreed to help Uther reach the fair Igraine. His aid would be given on one condition: that the child conceived that night would be entrusted to his care. In his haste, the king agreed. By his arts, Merlin transformed Uther into the likeness of the duke and that night the sage sent Uther into the castle posing as the returning duke. As the king lay with Igraine his men engaged in battle with the duke and his followers. The duke died in the battle, and this would plague Uther's conscience all of his days. Not wishing to be reminded of this, the child conceived in the shadow of the duke's death was given to Merlin as promised. Seemingly out of nowhere, Merlin appeared to claim the infant Arthur; then, child in arm, he disappeared beyond the horizon.

Throughout Arthur's early days Merlin would often appear at crucial moments and then, with an air of mystery, retreat again into his wilderness. In this sense Merlin was a bringer of the future, at times even its architect, manipulating events to ensure the healing of his torn land.

2. THE PRIESTESS
Ruled by the Moon

NIMUE

MEANING

A deep stirring within the self. A subtle but powerful connection with the collective unconscious or world soul. An inspired state of being. Surges of wisdom that benefit any creative endeavour, artistic, esoteric, or scientific.

Seeking guidance and knowledge. Seclusion and self-reliance. Good judgement and astute psychic ability. Feminine principles and grace. A need for solitude. Creating a receptive state of mind. Meditation brings new solutions to light.

REVERSED

Dormant talents and wisdom. The waste or misuse of skills and knowledge. Lack of inspiration; hollow existence. A negative influence affecting emotional stability and impairing judgement. Being deceived by a superficial show of knowledge. Ignorance and an unwillingness to consider the advice of others.

DESCRIPTION AND SYMBOLISM

The priestess Nimue and her company congregate in a sacred grove. She is one of the priestesses of Avalon—envoys of the Goddess and bearers of ancient wisdom. In the woods Nimue is surrounded by the spirits of nature. Unlike the Empress who is crowned by the people, here the Priestess is crowned by the Fay. Intensely curious, they cannot help but touch her, drape themselves about her, and play in her hair. After all, although she is sensitive to them, she is not of them. This represents her active relationship with the unseen and higher planes. Magnetic and mysterious, a skilled healer and adviser, she is also respected in the world of people—the priestess walks in both worlds. Nimue is wrapped in an iridescent cloak of light, representing her enlightened state of being. The surroundings and her dress are predominantly dark blue and purple, the colours of mystic knowledge. The book which traditionally lies in the lap of the Priestess has been replaced here by the flame which hovers between her hands, symbolic of her receptivity. Though she is educated in the ways of the Old Gods, hers is an art which cannot strictly be learned through labour. She is by her very nature a conductor of this energy; this is an inherent ability which raises her to the office of Priestess.

NIMUE

imue is one of several women to hold the title Chief Damsel of the Lake. This can lead to some confusion, as the name Lady of the Lake may refer to, among others, Morgan, or the water spirit who fosters Lancelot and rises from the waters to give and later receive Excalibur.

Nimue is most often remembered as Merlin's undoing. The sage first happened upon her while she was dancing in the woods. As he watched her graceful movements he felt his heart twist and recognized the danger, but was powerless to stop the emotion that overcame him and clouded his mind. From that day on Merlin followed her everywhere. Though he was always at her heels, Nimue dared not rebuke the great Merlin for fear of his wrath and magical powers. The indignant court marvelled at the sight of their wisest counsellor acting the fool, and the gossip began. Arthur was thus relieved when Merlin announced that they would be leaving the court to travel through Brittany and Cornwall. Nimue had agreed to accompany Merlin on the condition that he promise not to use his powers to overcome her. Nimue, meanwhile, had promised herself that she would learn all she could of Merlin's magic arts so that one day she might be rid of him.

Merlin's obsession deepened with time, and his relentless advances took a sinister turn. Nimue had waited as long as she dared. Aided by the enchantment he had taught her, Nimue trapped Merlin in a cave where he would remain for all eternity. Some say he languishes in a tower of air or under a great stone. Others believe he was not trapped at all, but merely chose to retire to the Isle of the Otherworld. In this interpretation of their relationship, Nimue was a trusted escort and nurse, a companion to help him on his journey to the twilight realm.

Whether Merlin had simply withdrawn, become dangerous, or gone mad (a common fate of his kind), it seems whatever action Nimue had taken was considered justified, as there were no serious repercussions beyond gossip when she returned to the court. Nimue became an important advisor and friend to the king, saving his life and guarding him from the treachery of his sister. Nimue was also a great source of comfort to the knight Pellas, when the lady he had been courting slept with Gawain. The

Lady Ettard had not taken the affections of Pellas seriously, as she had led him to believe. Rather she thought herself capable of securing a husband of higher standing. Nimue cast a spell on Ettard which induced her to love Pellas. By this time, however, it was too late. Pellas had not only recovered from his despair, but also had come to trust and love Nimue. In time, Pellas and the honoured Damsel of the Lake were married.

3. THE EMPRESS
RULED BY VENUS

GUENEVERE

MEANING

Beauty, intelligence, and spiritual strength. Renewal, creativity, and good public relations. A wise and decisive businesswoman. Maternal feelings and fertility. A kind and charitable woman who instils confidence and nurtures others.

An accomplished person with an appreciation of the arts. A responsible, active member of the community. Self-sacrifice for the benefit of others. Peace and harmony, motherhood, progress, and prosperity. An admirable woman and inspirational role model who adheres to her own values.

REVERSED

Domestic turmoil. Extravagance, insecurity, and lack of fulfilment. Overly protective behaviour. Infertility or an unwanted pregnancy. Unhealthy suppression of emotions. Engaging in secret activities or passionate fantasies to relieve monotony.

DESCRIPTION AND SYMBOLISM

The throne looms over Guenevere, representing the tremendous responsibility of the High Queen. Despite the youth of Arthur's bride, she possesses a regal air and is capable of rising to the occasion. With flowers in her hair and a dress of green, she is the May Queen, a figure of renewal and fertility. The apple blossoms are symbolic of the Goddess and represent the process of regeneration. The brown and green colours of the throne and dress correspond to earth and vegetation respectively, bringing to mind the nurturing image of Mother Nature. As May Queen, Guenevere is responsible for the welfare of both her people and the land; a position which demands maturity, wisdom, and, if necessary, self-sacrifice. The purple cloak denotes royalty, leadership, and privileged class. The eagle represents the strength that comes of enlightenment—she has the ability to rise above a situation and take definitive action. The harp at her side symbolizes her attraction to things of beauty; she is an appreciative and generous patron of the arts. In contrast to the Priestess who sits outside, Guenevere sits inside a great hall; she reigns in the world of people, business, and politics. The Empress is co-ruler, the equal feminine counterpart to the Emperor.

GUENEVERE

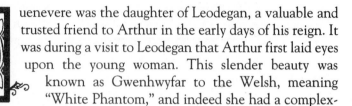

uenevere was the daughter of Leodegan, a valuable and trusted friend to Arthur in the early days of his reign. It was during a visit to Leodegan that Arthur first laid eyes upon the young woman. This slender beauty was known as Gwenhwyfar to the Welsh, meaning "White Phantom," and indeed she had a complex-ion of cream and the grace of a swan. Arthur had made his choice, though Merlin disapproved and warned that Guenevere would bring him much sorrow.

In some versions of the Arthurian saga, Guenevere is seen as a tragic figure; in others she is blamed for the failure of Arthur's vision. Her affair with Lancelot was said to have caused a division among the Knights of the Round Table. Since she was the wife of the High King, Guene-vere's relationship with Arthur's best friend was considered not only adul-tery, but also an act of high treason, punishable by death (see Eight of Swords). Although Arthur tried to overlook this indiscretion, the people and their new ways demanded justice. Lancelot would have to oppose the king and break the Fellowship to save his love.

This rather harsh treatment of Guenevere may be the result of interpretations by Christian chroniclers of medieval society. In reality, Guenevere's taking of lovers would not have been considered such a dire sin. The land was in a state of religious transition, a time when Celtic pre-Christian and Christian values overlapped. The old ways gave the queen complete equality with all the same rights and powers as the king. The Celtic queen was involved in all aspects of rule, including war. What the warrior queens may have lacked in brawn, they often made up in skill and strategic planning. Medb of Ireland provides a fine example of this, as does the famous Boudicca (or Boadicea) of Britain, to whom a monument stands on the Thames Embankment. These Celtic queens were within their right to take lovers, as did their counterparts, the kings. We see this practice with Morgause, among others, and in the attitudes of the Lady of the Lake who tells Guenevere that there is nothing wrong with her love for Lancelot. In some versions of the story the affair with Lancelot is mentioned only in passing, if at all.

Apart from differing depictions of her infidelity, the portrayal of Guenevere also varies radically from that of a cold queen who treated the knights with contempt to that of a generous, much-loved queen who nurtured the Fellowship. Contradictions also arise as to the fertility of the queen. While most present Guenevere as barren, the Welsh tradition insists that she did give birth to Arthur's sons. The health and fertility of the queen were important considerations, as it was believed they were directly linked with the state of the land itself. The custom of Maying embodied this sentiment.

Each year Guenevere would ride out on May Day to welcome the season. Knowing this, the love-struck Melwas, ruler of the Summer Land, planned to abduct the queen as she roamed the woods. Melwas lay in wait and watched as the queen and her party of green adorned themselves with flowers, herbs, and mosses and danced in the early sunshine. Seeing his opportunity, Melwas rose up, snatched Guenevere, and was gone. Word reached Arthur (or in some accounts, Lancelot) that the queen had been abducted and was being held by Melwas. The abductor's home was Glastonbury Tor in Somerset, a favourite haunt of the Faery. The hill was surrounded by an "adventurous marsh" which made rescue difficult. Nevertheless, Arthur led his troops on from Cornwall and Devon, ready to risk all-out war for his queen. The monk Gildas and a local abbot, however, were not. They were able to intercede and negotiate the return of Guenevere, thus preserving the peace.

4. THE EMPEROR
RULED BY ARIES

ARTHUR

MEANING

Wisdom and power. A mature man of distinction. A caring person with many responsibilities. Conquest and conviction. Courage and ambition balanced with reason and fair play.

A competitive nature. Rising to meet a challenge. Achievement and competence. One who is open to the ideas and counsel of others. A strong masculine influence. Impressive leadership when faced with a threatening situation. Progress and security. Established authority. Creating a stable, protective environment. Reason ruling emotion; adherence to the laws of society.

REVERSED

Immaturity. Inability to cope with responsibility. Feeble efforts. Subservience and hypocrisy. An inability to make difficult decisions causes others to lose faith. The display of petty behaviour.

DESCRIPTION AND SYMBOLISM

A confident Arthur sits in the seat of power. He is comfortable, yet aware of his surroundings and his crucial role. Arthur holds the sceptre and orb, confirmations of his sovereignty. The sceptre also symbolizes his potency; the orb his fame and feminine principles. Arthur's relaxed body language makes him seem approachable. His competence to rule is that of a true king, not a fallacy of pomp and ceremony. The king's capacity to rule comes from deep within him, a truth and strength which seem to hang in the very air around him. The light of the torch falls upon the king, recalling that he is an enlightened leader. His rich robe denotes wealth and security. The colour red, coupled with the shield, represents courage and his readiness to defend his kingdom. The eagle symbolizes the soul and his ability to rise above a situation, see both sides, and make a fair judgement. The ram heads represent his stamina, passion, and ambition. The dragons carved in the back of the throne symbolize primitive power. Arthur is the Pendragon ("Head Dragon") who vows a sacred marriage to the land. Though Arthur is loved by his people, he is also envied—the open door indicates that there are those who, if given the opportunity, would have his crown. The king must be aware of all that occurs in his court, and all that is done in his name.

ARTHUR

ost historians now agree that Arthur—or the man we call Arthur—did exist, if not as king, then at least as a military leader. He was a magnetic man and military mastermind whose warband grew with his fame. Arthur is probably the general who led the Britons to victory at the famous Battle of Mount Badon. With this decisive victory, the invading Saxons were kept at bay, bringing relative peace to the land. Thus, the title of king was likely bestowed upon the heroic Arthur by the storytellers of the grateful isle. They would also add to his fame and grandeur with a wealth of fantastic tales.

Our romanticized Arthur of legend was born to Uther and Igraine at Tintagel in Cornwall. The newborn was given to Merlin as part of a pact between the magician and the king. Merlin then placed the young Arthur in the foster care of Sir Ector. Here, with his foster brother Kay, Arthur received an education and learned the arts of war. Despite thinking himself someone's unwanted bastard, these were happy, carefree days for Arthur.

When the time came for Arthur to succeed his father, Merlin arranged for the nobles to meet for a tournament. Though there had been rumours that Uther had fathered a son, no one was certain of his existence. The tournament's victors won the right to attempt to pull a sword from a stone. This was a rite by which the people believed the Gods made known the rightful king of the land. It was in this setting, with all eyes upon him, that the 15-year-old Arthur pulled the sword from the stone. Merlin then told Arthur, and the dazed onlookers, that he was the child of the High King Uther Pendragon and his queen Igraine.

In the early days of his reign, Arthur remained under the watchful eye of Merlin, successfully overcoming the initial opposition of some disgruntled lesser kings and setting out to unite his fellow countrymen against the Saxon threat. Despite his youth, Arthur was an exemplary warrior and as time wore on he proved to be a great leader, dispelling any doubts regarding his prowess and authority. Arthur was a fair and courageous man, but capable of making harsh decisions when necessary. His warlike nature was balanced with kindness and humour. His talent for verse (particularly satirical verse) made him a favourite among the bards.

The early battles of Arthur and his warband were severe but successful, culminating with the victory of Mount Badon. The now confident (and perhaps somewhat jealous) Arthur announced that he would dig up the head of Bran which lay buried on Tower Hill in London. The people believed Bran's head to be a talisman protecting the isle from outsiders, while to Arthur it was a long-dead competitor, mere superstition, and a thorn in his side. He asserted that it was his campaign, not a charm, that protected the land. Arthur exhumed the head, thereby declaring his own supremacy. This act did not sit well with everyone and some would blame later troubles on this misdeed.

The king then turned his attention to rebuilding and reorganizing the country. At this time he married Guenevere, who some maintain was his second wife. Welsh tradition names three sons of Arthur: Llacheu, Gwydre, and Amr. It is not known whether Llacheu was legitimate, but Gwydre and Amr were not, and all died before their father. According to legend, Guenevere brought Arthur the Round Table, which had belonged to Uther, as part of her dowry. The Round Table held both a mystical and a practical appeal, unifying all while honouring no man above the rest. With this, The Fellowship of the Round Table was born. And so began the many (too many to recount here!) adventures of King Arthur and the Knights of the Table Round.

5. THE HIEROPHANT
RULED BY TAURUS

TALIESIN

MEANING

A person with experience he or she is willing to share. An authority. A kind and generous mentor who nurtures a spiritual awareness. A medium to a higher plane. Advocate of tradition. Blessings, education, religious ceremony. Initiation. Drawing comfort and security from one's roots. Laying a foundation for a belief system. Encouragement to explore the framework of a religion or doctrine. Feeling constricted by the attitudes of society as a whole. Pressure to live up to the expectations of others.

The traditional interpretation of the card is orthodox behaviour, conforming to a system or organization.

REVERSED

Rigid thinking with no room for growth. Withholding or distorting information to retain power. Intolerance and propaganda. Mistaken moral superiority as a justification for the persecution of others. Obtaining obedience through fear rather than trust. Inherited prejudices. Gullibility.

DESCRIPTION AND SYMBOLISM

Taliesin introduces the children to his lady—the harp. Orpheus charmed his way to the underworld and back by way of his music. Music is a passage to the Otherworld and this is why the harp has been substituted for the keys traditionally found in the hand of the Hierophant.

Taliesin encourages questions from the royal and less privileged children alike. He fosters their creative, artistic talents and passes on the age-old lore, providing the children with a foundation for their own flights of fancy. By investing in the children's imagination and awakening their talents, the stories of the past will live on and the connection with the Otherworld (and its guides) will continue. This is Taliesin's charge as custodian of the ancient lore.

The feathers in his hair and the necklace strung with tokens of his incarnations attest to his renowned shapeshifting abilities. The bard embodies all the knowledge of these animal lives. Like Merlin, Taliesin has a close connection with the Old Ones. The stream and the stone figures of the Old Gods reflect this bond. It is through his connection with the Otherworldly, particularly the Cauldron of Ceridwen, that he acquires his inspiration and profound knowledge. The jewelry he wears speaks of the affection and respect he is granted; his patron rewards him well for his services. The political power of this famed Welsh bard could not be underestimated. Through his craft he could bestow a king with an honoured place in history or destroy him with scorching satire.

TALIESIN

aliesin was a sixth-century poet and one of the five chief bards of the Isle of the Mighty. Twelve poems attributed to him have survived to the present day, some of which are thought to be authentic. Although it is considered too late to be Taliesin's, the poem *The Spoils of Annwfn* connects him with Arthur and the raid on Annwn (see Six of Swords).

As with his contemporaries, fantastic tales have naturally grown up around Taliesin. Our story begins with the bard as a young boy named Gwion. The great witch Ceridwen assigned him the task of tending her cauldron. For a year and a day he was to stir the magical brew. Ceridwen would then give the mixture, a source of great knowledge, to her son as compensation for his hideous appearance. As the fateful day drew near Gwion accidentally splashed himself with the brew. In licking three drops off his fingers he became the unintended recipient of the All Knowing, and thus became aware of Ceridwen's plans to kill him once he had served his purpose. What remained of the brew was now only poison and the enraged Ceridwen gave chase. With his newly acquired gifts Gwion shifted his shape to that of a hare. Ceridwen followed in the shape of a greyhound. He took to a stream, becoming a fish; Ceridwen followed as an otter. He took to the air as a small bird; she followed as a hawk. Lastly, Gwion became a grain of wheat. Ceridwen, in the shape of a black hen, swallowed him. Returning to her own shape, Ceridwen was now pregnant with Gwion. In time, she gave birth to the child. On seeing his beauty, however, she could not bring herself to kill him, but set him adrift upon the sea in a leather bag. Elphin, the nephew of King Maelgwn, found the bag caught on a salmon weir. He carefully opened it and on seeing the child exclaimed, "Behold a radiant brow!" And so the child was named Taliesin, meaning "Radiant Brow." Elphin's family took him into their care and raised him.

Taliesin's power first attracted attention when he journeyed to the court of King Maelgwn to rescue his imprisoned patron Elphin. To avoid interference from the haughty resident bards, Taliesin cast a spell upon them so that the only words they could speak were "blerwn, blerwn." To add to their indignity, the enchantment also caused them to compulsively finger their bottom lips. Under the disdainful glare of the king, the chief bard, Heinin, strained against the spell. After what seemed an eternity, Heinin managed to blurt out that they were not drunk, as it seemed, but were under a spell cast by the boy in the corner! Now commanding the king's undivided attention, Taliesin stepped forward. The king asked him who he was, and in reply Taliesin began to recite his now famous poem of "I Have Beens," recounting his many incarnations. With the sound of his voice the chains that held Elphin fell away. Taliesin then began to foretell the future of Britain. As he spoke the wind rose until it raged, shaking the hall and nearly drowning his words. As the prophesies drew to a close the wind subsided, leaving all quiet but for the whispered chants of the bards.

6. THE LOVERS
Ruled by Gemini

GARETH & LYONES

MEANING

The blossoming of a valuable and balanced relationship, intimate though not necessarily sexual. A dance; a connection on a higher level. Infatuation. Mutual understanding and deep emotions.

Harmonious flow of energy lending a sense of ease and comfort. Trust and free will.

Depending on the neighbouring cards, it may indicate a choice to be made between what is desired and what is acceptable. The help and support of a lover.

REVERSED

Pining for a past relationship. Obsessive romantic or sexual fantasies dominating one's life. An unbalanced relationship; one in which one partner is vulnerable, subject to the whims of the other, or one in which one side remains detached, unable to give or receive love.

DESCRIPTION AND SYMBOLISM

Gareth and Lyones walk alone in the woods, far from the curious eyes and gossip of the court. They walk together, but do not cling to one another. Theirs is a secure love of equal partners who choose each other's company of their own free will. A warm breeze flows through the leaves of the trees, reflecting the gentle nature of the love and affection Gareth and Lyones have for one another. The peacock butterflies symbolize the beauty and ecstasy of this dusty, dreamlike state.

The sword is a reminder that there are dangers amidst this beauty. Though love can exalt, when lost it can devastate. This was a truth familiar to the Arthurian lovers. Despite the veneer of romance, they did not live fairy-tale lives—theirs was a dangerous and violent age (see Eight of Swords). In the context of the card, the sword symbolizes the hazards of collapsing into a relationship and the need to retain one's sense of self and independence. To do otherwise would be unhealthy for both partners and drain the strength needed to survive the twists of fate in worldly life. The love of Gareth and Lyones was a true love—rare and unfailing. The goldenrod blooms in the foreground, symbolizing the natural union (goldenrod = solidago, "to join").

GARETH & LYONES

areth of Orkney was the younger brother of Gawain, Agravain, and Gaheris. When he first came to Camelot he kept his identity secret, wishing to prove himself by his own deeds rather than relying on his relationship to the famous Gawain. During this time he was known only as Beaumains, a nickname given to him by Kay, meaning "fair hands." As Beaumains, he patiently worked in the kitchens, awaiting an opportunity to prove himself. This he eventually did by rescuing the Lady Lyones, who for two years had been a hostage of the knight Ironside. While witnessing the ensuing battle, Lyones fell deeply in love with her young, valiant champion, and he with her, giving him the strength to prevail (see the Hanged Man).

The two later met amid the celebrations held at the castle of Lyones' brother, Gringamore. There was great cheer, dancing, games, fine wine, and meats, but Gareth was so fervoured by his love that he could not bring himself to eat. He watched every move Lyones made, his love deepening by the moment. Seeing how Gareth burned in his love, Gringamore sought to ease his agony. Knowing that his sister's love for Gareth equalled that of her young champion, Gringamore told him so. There was never a happier man than Gareth. With Gringamore's assurance, Gareth then spoke with Lyones who vowed that her love for him would last all her days. The two made plans to meet later that night, once all the guests had retired. Lyones instructed Gareth to sleep in the hall and she would join him just before midnight. It became clear to all present that the two were deeply in love. The enchantress Linet, sister to Lyones, suspected their lusty intentions, and although she approved of their love, she hoped to delay their union until they were married. That night Lyones secretly made her way through the castle to join Gareth in his bed. Meanwhile, Linet conjured up a phantom knight whom she sent to attack Gareth at this delicate moment. The battle was fierce, leaving Linet's knight decapitated and Gareth exhausted with a badly wounded thigh. Gringamore, awakened by Lyones' screams, rushed to help, and joined the two lovers just as Linet entered the room. The enchantress calmly walked up to her knight, applied an ointment to his neck, placed his head back upon his shoulders, and restored him to life, warning the lovers to cool their hot blood until they were wed. Ten days passed and despite Gareth's wound their yearning for one another drove them to plan a second meeting. Lyones had not been in Gareth's bed long when she saw the brilliant light of the phantom knight approaching. With sword at his bedside, Gareth was prepared for the knight's timely interruption. As their battle escalated, so too did the ghostly light; its blaze became so bright that Lyones was blind to the struggle. Gareth's wound reopened and the loss of blood weakened him, but he was eventually triumphant, again beheading the phantom knight. This time Gareth chopped the head into a hundred pieces and threw them out a nearby window. Linet diligently gathered these, however, piecing her knight back together and restoring him to duty. Gareth suffered with his wound, preventing any further mischief, but Linet told the angry young lover that when the time came she would heal him and restore him to his healthy, lustful self. At long last the day came when—honour intact—the two were wed and their ordeal with the phantom chaperone ceased.

7. THE CHARIOT
RULED BY CANCER

BATTLE OF MOUNT BADON

MEANING

Triumph, victory. Leadership of a large organized effort. Dedication to a cause. Defensive strength; control or direction of turmoil. Maturity. Possessing the strength of one's convictions. A need to remain focused and keep emotions in check. Conscious effort to overcome (if only temporarily) internal conflict in order to accomplish the task at hand. Controlling a situation of conflicting sentiments. Overcoming obstacles through perseverance and strength of will.

REVERSED

The collapse of an enterprise. Defeat; loss of focus. The ambiguity that weakens defenses. Lack of confidence; captivity to one's own fears. Potential to be led astray. A lack of concern for others undermines leadership.

DESCRIPTION AND SYMBOLISM

Arthur's seasoned warriors follow him into battle. The great speed of the chariot reflects the accelerated rate at which events unfold. There is a need at such moments of excitement to keep a cool head and harness one's emotions. This self-control is symbolized by the horses. The black and white represent the polarities of the mind and their occasionally conflicting qualities: logic and emotion; passion and reason. The horses reflect this distinction—though not in total harmony; they are under the driver's control. No doubt this dichotomy must have plagued the men of Mount Badon. Their hearts wished to avoid the horrors of war, yet reason asserted that the invaders be driven back and boundaries be protected if they were to prevent future bloodshed.

The driver is in touch with his intuitive side, symbolized by the lunar crescents that adorn his shoulders. The armoured shell of the horses echoes the card's connection with the zodiac sign of Cancer. A strong sense of shared identity is symbolized by the standard, crowning the scene and reflecting the promise of glory.

BATTLE OF MOUNT BADON

y the time of Arthur, the Imperial system in Britain had collapsed. In its place stood a threadbare administrative system. Facing the threat of three invading nations, Britain appealed to Rome for help, only to be told she must fend for herself. The Picts and the Irish Scotti tribes raided the northern borders and western shores, while the Angles, Jutes, and Saxons invaded the eastern and southern shores. Of all these, the Saxon advance was the greatest threat. It was said that their cruel ways terrorized the people of the land. Such a desperate historical context calls for and gives rise to many heroic deeds, both real and fictitious, and the Battle of Mount Badon would secure Arthur's place as a legendary, titanic leader.

Although the exact date is unknown, we do know that this battle would have occurred around the year A.D. 500. Archaeological evidence suggests that at this approximate time the Saxon advance was halted. It is said that a measure of Arthur's success was due to his revival of the cavalry, loosely based on the Imperial model. Not only did the horse lend the advantages of speed and mobility, but the sight of mounted soldiers had a powerful psychological effect on an enemy fighting on foot. Battle dress varied according to what an individual could afford: the opulent were protected by leather jerkins, chain mail, and helmets; the rest depended upon breast and back plates of leather. The British warriors carried long swords and relied heavily on spears.

The earliest known reference to the siege of Mount Badon can be found in *De Excidio Britanniae* ("On the Ruin of Britain"), authored by a monk named Gildas who wrote within the lifetime of some of the battle veterans, approximately A.D. 530. Although this work acknowledges the achievement at Badon, it does not name the leader of the British force. It is in the collection of twelfth-century manuscripts known as *Historia Brittonum* ("History of the Britons") that Arthur is first identified as this leader. This work is commonly attributed to Nennius, a monk of north Wales, who transcribed and compiled many earlier texts to create the *Historia*. We learn from the *Historia* that Badon was the twelfth battle of Arthur and his warband. Continuing for three days and nights, it was to be Arthur's greatest triumph.

Geoffrey of Monmouth draws on the *Historia* in creating his idealized history of Britain, *The History of the Kings of Britain*. In this account, Arthur carried his famous sword Caliburn and his spear Ron, rallied his men, and attacked the vast army of Saxons. Both sides fought bravely. Arthur lost many men in his effort to take the hill and there seemed no end to the battle on the summit. Seeing that the enemy still held fast, Arthur raised up Caliburn, cried out to the higher powers, and plunged deep into the ranks of the enemy. Arthur's battle frenzy inspired his men, who followed him with renewed vigour. At this point the battle turned in Arthur's favour and the Britons went on to victory. Legend rewards these brave veterans with a generation of relative peace.

8. STRENGTH
RULED BY LEO

PERCIVALE'S VISION

MEANING

Having the courage and vitality to realize one's goals. Ambition tempered with serenity—a gentle strength. Intelligence and reason united with enthusiasm and energy. Discipline; channeling one's passions in a constructive way. Having the strength of convictions. Drawing on resources of inner strength to resist temptation. Listening to the inner voice for direction. Understanding the consequences of one's actions.

REVERSED

Loss of courage; abandoning one's own values. Being driven by impulses. Unjustified use of strength. Resorting to intimidation in an effort to manipulate and control others. Being seduced into dismissing one's own code of conduct.

DESCRIPTION AND SYMBOLISM

Physical prowess and intelligence unite. The Maid aspect of the Goddess rides the lion. She is blossoming into adulthood, and as yet unjaded, she brings enthusiasm and a love of life to the card. Through her kindness she has won the lion's confidence and benefits from its strength and courage.

The Crone aspect of the Goddess rides the serpent. Though the Hebrew name for Strength is "serpent," it seems that most often its presence is overshadowed by the glory of the lion. Here it is portrayed as an equal partner, bringing wisdom and the Crone's experience to the card. This symbolizes strength and energy with direction.

The two women link hands, combining their assets. This represents someone using all of their potential: motivating passion and navigating mind.

PERCIVALE'S VISION

ir Thomas Malory's *Le Morte d'Arthur* is the reference for the following story of Percivale's Vision. It is worth bearing in mind that the book was written in a pious age, when old stories were often modified to reflect prevailing views. Hence, the young woman and the lion come to represent Christianity, while the Crone and serpent represent Paganism and the devil. If the Gods and Goddesses of the former religion could not make a smooth transition into a Christian guise, they were doomed to become fiends and enemies of the new religion. Knowing this, despite the story's semblance of Christianity, we can recognize the early Pagan Goddess in her guise of Maid and Crone testing Percivale's strength and dedication to the Quest. The Goddess tests Gawain's fortitude and conviction in much the same way in the stories of Ragnell (see Nine of Shields) and the Green Knight (see Ten of Spears). Now, without further ado, we shall join Percivale in the wilds.

In Percivale's Quest for the Holy Grail, he finds himself marooned on an island wilderness of beasts. On seeing a great battle between a lion and a serpent, Percivale killed the serpent, judging the lion to be the gentler of the two. This won him a great friend in the grateful lion. That night Percivale dreamt of two women: one young and beautiful, riding a lion; the other old and wizened, riding a serpent. The Maid warned Percivale that on the morrow he would do battle with the strongest of champions, and should he fail he would be shamed till the world's end. With that, she disappeared. Then the Crone spoke of the serpent he had killed, claiming it belonged to her. In order to make amends, she suggested that he become her man. Percivale refused. Thereupon she assured him that she would find him "without keeping" and that he would be hers.

The next day a spectre of an old man appeared to Percivale and counseled him to be true of heart and to the order of chivalry. He explained to Percivale that lion and young woman represented the new law of the holy church, faith, good hope, belief, and baptism. He then went on to say that she who rode the serpent betokened the old law, and was a powerful fiend. With that, he vanished.

At midday, a ship carrying a beautiful woman approached the island. The damsel told Percivale she had been disinherited and banished from the court, but despite this, many knights remained loyal and followed her. The sympathetic Percivale promised to help her, and in turn she agreed to feed the starving knight and help him off the isle.

The young woman ordered her pavilion to be set up, and then gave Percivale his fill of fine meats and the strongest of wine. The more time he spent in her company, the more infatuated Percivale became. He swore she was the finest creature ever and prayed that she be his. The damsel refused. Percivale continued to plead, and at long last an agreement was made: Percivale swore by the faith of his body to serve only her, and do only as she commanded, and in turn she agreed to fulfil his lusty desires. While the eager Percivale awaited her undressing, he glimpsed the crucifix on the pommel of his sword. Remembering his Quest and the old man's words, he made the sign of the cross on his forehead. With this, the pavilion whirled upside down and vanished in a cloud of smoke. And so she too "went with the wind," all the while roaring of his betrayal. Having nearly succumbed to temptation, Percivale believed himself unworthy of the Quest for the Holy Grail. In a moment of despair he drove his sword through his thigh, thinking to punish the flesh that ruled him. All hope was not lost as Percivale had thought. The old man who had appeared to Percivale before his trial returned with a ship. As wind and wave carried them from the isle the old man explained that the beautiful seductress and the old woman were one and the same—the devil.

9. THE HERMIT
RULED BY VIRGO

LANCELOT IN EXILE

MEANING

A need for solitude. Caring for the soul. Recuperating and slowly centering one's self. Cherishing time alone. Examining one's true feelings. Consulting the wisdom within. A need to pay close attention to dreams and the poignant teachings they can embody.

Traditionally, the Hermit can represent a meeting with a wise person who may aid one's search, but ultimately the answers one seeks must be found within; only then can they be fully realized.

REVERSED

Rejecting assistance from others. Fear and suspicion of the outside world prevents worthwhile interactions. An unwillingness to explore new ideas. The search for self-knowledge has been hampered by brooding and depression. Dismissing sound advice.

DESCRIPTION AND SYMBOLISM

Lancelot flees the turmoil of court life. The forest symbolizes a safe and private environment in which to recuperate. Here, resembling a wildman, he is free. Dropping all masks and pretenses he is closer to his true self and can begin his search of the soul.

The roots of the tree symbolize a need to examine the health of one's foundation in order to find what has been weakened by neglect. In the stillness of the Hermit we tend to the needs of the mind and soul— for when the strong winds blow it is the strength of the roots that ensures the tree's survival.

Lancelot carries a torch in his left hand, indicating the subconscious at work, guiding and illuminating the way. This is a reminder to watch for the insights carried in dreams.

The spring depicted in the painting lies in the west country of England; it is believed to be of great antiquity and today carries the name of St. Ambrew's Well. Many springs were thought to have curative powers and here, deep within the tangled forest, Lancelot finds the door that guards the sacred spring. This symbolizes a return to a long forgotten source of inspiration and spiritual fulfilment.

LANCELOT IN EXILE

ancelot du Lac was the flower of chivalry; a role model to many knights and the passion of many women.

King Pelles had a beautiful daughter, known as Elaine of Corbenic, who was desperately in love with Lancelot. Unlike the other women of the court, Elaine was not deterred by Lancelot's love for the queen. Any chance that they could be together lay with the magical arts of Elaine's lady-in-waiting. Brisen was an enchantress who foresaw that the child of Lancelot's and Elaine's union, Galahad, could benefit the land. And so Brisen led Lancelot to Elaine's chambers and there made him believe that Guenevere awaited him inside.

As Lancelot lay with Elaine, Guenevere sent her lady-in-waiting to fetch him. When the maid reported that she found his bed cold, Guenevere flew into a rage. Suspecting Elaine, she raced to her chambers where the two were found sleeping. In her fury, Guenevere banished both from the court. It was only then that Lancelot realized he had been deceived (or so he said). Lancelot was so grieved by Guenevere's words that he fell to the floor in a swoon. On awakening, he was quite out of his wits. Wearing only a shirt, he leapt out of the window and ran to the protection of the forest.

For two years Lancelot remained in the sanctuary of the woods, running with the animals and feeding on berries. The Knights of the Round Table searched for their friend to no avail. Though there were sightings, no one recognized the wildman as Lancelot du Lac until Elaine came upon him sleeping by a well. She immediately sent news of her find to King Pelles—guardian of the Grail. And so, by the virtue of the Grail, Lancelot's mind was healed.

10. WHEEL OF FORTUNE
RULED BY JUPITER

ARTHUR'S DREAM

MEANING

Change of fortune. Karma. The beginning or end of a cycle. Good luck. Destiny. An arising chance for growth and development. Riding a wave of success. Fortuitous timing. Seeds planted in the past come to harvest. A need to recognize a window of opportunity, as it is only temporarily available, and will disappear with the inevitable turn of the wheel.

REVERSED

Trying times. Feeling frustrated with the inability to influence a difficult situation. Being held back by lack of opportunity.

An unforseen bad turn of events forces one to ride out the storm. Having to contend with insecurity that breeds a strong attachment to the past and makes change painful.

DESCRIPTION AND SYMBOLISM

Favoured by Fortuna, Arthur sits atop the wheel. From this vantage point Arthur can see all that is happening, and with this knowledge his mind can soar. The privilege of this enlightenment is represented by the wings of spiritual flight.

The Round Table forms the wheel, symbolizing the perpetual motion of the psyche and experiences of life.

The water is the subconscious and the serpents represent our deep-rooted fears which lurk here.

Past experience with the downturn of the wheel can shake our confidence, leaving psychological wounds, particularly insecurity and mistrust of fortune. These fears inhibit our efforts to climb, as represented by the creature who claws at the rising man.

The floating bodies remind us that Fortuna is not always fair. She is blind, and in spinning her wheel she sometimes rewards the unworthy while neglecting the needy.

Though we never come to understand the temperamental moods of Fortuna, we all are subject to her wheel of hope, glory, regret, and despair.

ARTHUR'S DREAM

ordred had raised an army against his father, the king. On the eve of this last battle, Arthur had a dreadful dream. He found himself lost in a wood of wild beasts. All about him they feasted on the bodies of his dead knights. Terrorized by the sight, Arthur ran until he reached a clearing. It was a gentle meadow covered with clover and wildflowers. Shepherds tended the flocks under an avenue of trees where silver vines hung heavy with grapes.

From within the clouds appeared a beautiful woman dressed in embroidered silk and ribbons of gold. In her hand she carried a wheel which she occasionally spun. A fine chair was fastened to this wheel and below it, clinging to the rim, were two kings. Both were as white as chalk as they desperately tried to reach the chair. The man closest to the chair wore a cloak of silver embroidered with crosses of gold, while the other wore a cloak of blue decorated with gold fleurs de lys.

Fortuna picked up Arthur and set him upon the chair. She then fed him all manner of fruits and wine, asking that he drink to her. Fortuna showed him much affection, but with time she took on a menacing mood and began to threaten the king. Arthur became aware of deep water below him in which hideous serpents spat and thrashed about. With the words "Thou shalt lose this game" Fortuna suddenly spun her wheel. In his fall from grace Arthur crushed his jaw, while the spinning wheel broke the rest of his bones, leaving him to be torn apart by the monstrous worms. The terrified Arthur awoke, but soon drifted into a half sleep. In this state the ghost of Gawain appeared to him and warned him not to fight the following day—for if he did he would surely die (see Ten of Swords).

11. JUSTICE
RULED BY LIBRA

LADY OF THE LAKE

MEANING

Justice delivers total honesty and reveals the consequences of past actions. It represents receiving one's just rewards. Achieving balance and harmony after toils and tribulations. Responsible conduct. Reaching a state of equilibrium with one's self. Peace of mind. Making a well-balanced choice. Entering into an equal partnership. Being able to see both sides of a situation. Integrity and contracts. Reaching an agreement. The favourable outcome of a judicial matter.

REVERSED

Dishonest dealings with others. Judgement clouded by prejudice. Unjust conduct or decisions. Not being truthful with one's self. Denying the true motivations for one's actions. Abuse. Being mired down in complex legal matters.

DESCRIPTION AND SYMBOLISM

The Lady of the Lake appears to Arthur, representing cosmic law. She is a reminder that there is a mightier court than the king's justice.

In light of his past deeds the Lady of the Lake deems him worthy of her seal, presenting him with Excalibur and the scabbard.

Her figure embodies the scales of justice as she weighs the virtues of sword and scabbard. The determination and decisive actions of the sword are in equilibrium with the mercy and protection of the scabbard. This represents a well-balanced person who can be entrusted to carry out responsibilities in an honourable manner.

The appearance of the Lady of the Lake signifies the workings of destiny and karma. For this reason, a sense of order and peace accompany this card's presence.

Arthur represents a person who has matured and followed both his destiny and conscience and now receives recognition.

LADY OF THE LAKE

ing Pellinore had made a camp in the forest not far from Arthur's court. There he challenged and bested each of Arthur's knights who passed his way. Pellinore found great amusement in his pastime, but Arthur's patience was wearing thin. And so he rose early one morning and rode alone (or so he thought) to meet this Pellinore and take up the challenge himself.

The battle was fierce and both were gravely wounded. Pellinore was a seasoned, valiant warrior and in his rage might have killed the young king. Hidden from view, Merlin recognized the danger and cast a spell which hung heavy on Pellinore, bringing him to the ground in a deep sleep. The king lay unconscious and his sword (that which he had pulled from the stone) lay in pieces. Merlin had Arthur moved to a hermitage to be healed of his wounds, leaving Pellinore to recover in peace. When well enough to travel, Merlin led the king on a journey far from the court. For many days they rode until they reached a strange and beautiful Land of Lakes. The magick of the place hung all about them, teasing at their sense of reality. Whispered words rode the wind: "the coming of Arthur draws near." One could sense the company of unseen escorts as they approached the calmest of lakes. Above its still waters a faint air of music danced with the mist. Never had Arthur seen such a place.

"Within the lake lies a rock, and within the rock a beautiful palace; this is the home of the Lady of the Lake. Speak fair to her," Merlin warned, "and she will honour you with a gift of sword and scabbard. The sword is like no other wielded by man; forged in the Otherworld, it is eternal. The scabbard is woven of magick; while you wear it no mortal injury will harm you."

With these words the mist lifted and the waters rose, giving form to a woman—the Lady was upon the Lake.

She held the king breathless within her gaze as she spoke. "Arthur, king, there lies within you the promise of peace in the land. For this reason I give you my sword. Excalibur will inspire others to follow you, while the scabbard will protect you from harm. This is my gift to further your cause. Take this offering, guard it well, and know you carry my blessing."

With Excalibur in the king's hands the waters breathed, reclaiming the figure that had been the Lady of the Lake. Once again, the mirror sheet hid all from view.

12. THE HANGED MAN
RULED BY NEPTUNE

CASTLE PERILOUS

MEANING

Restriction; self-sacrifice. Championing the noble cause of others. Feeling drained of energy and resources. Suspension of plans. Seeming to have no control over the events of one's life. A wise and sometimes temporary surrender in order to conserve energy. Enduring self-sacrifice as a part of initiation. The experience and teachings of recent trials renews a sense of peace and heightens the feeling of being alive. Intuition and psychic abilities are attuned through suspension.

REVERSED

Futile attempts to revive something that time has passed. Refusing to accept reality. A martyr on behalf of an empty cause. Not knowing when to retreat prolongs oppression and suffering. Psychological blocks undermine confidence and freeze all action. `

DESCRIPTION AND SYMBOLISM

The would-be champions of the Lady Lyones hang in the trees, unable to free her or themselves. As was the practice, both hands and one leg are bound behind their backs, representing restriction and limited power.

The battle wound and the stain mark the loss of blood, and represent weakening defenses; a reminder that energy levels are low. Despite a valiant struggle the road has been rough, putting a strain on resources, as symbolized by the damaged mail coat and twisted spurs.

Being hanged on a tree echoes the tale of the Norse God Odin, who hanged himself on the Tree of Life for nine days. He chose this disciplined act of self-sacrifice as a way to learn the secrets of the runes. The sensory deprivation which comes with restriction dampens the conscious mind producing an altered state in which one can gain profound insight. Rites of initiation often involved an act of self-sacrifice, such as fasting before a vision quest. This suggests that when no outward progress is possible, an inward journey would serve one well.

This is a time to examine old habits, as symbolized by the number of men who hang in the trees. All used the same tactics and outmoded thinking; a new approach would help.

The tree gathers moss and the mist lies low, telling of the stillness of the card. Action now is unlikely. The only life to flourish in this scene is the mandrake that sprouts at the foot of the tree. This plant was believed to mark the spot of a hanging.

CASTLE PERILOUS

ager to fight the most famous of Arthur's knights, Ironside the Red Knight of the Red Launde embattled himself in Castle Perilous, where he held the lovely Lady Lyones hostage. Confident that her plight would draw out the knights, Ironside patiently awaited their rescue attempts.

In the two years that passed, many a brave knight tried and failed to free the Lady Lyones. But still the famous opponents Ironside longed to face—Lancelot, Gawain, and Tristram—had not come. Linet, sister to Lyones, travelled to Arthur's court and requested that the king send a Knight of the Round Table to save her sister.

Arthur assigned Gareth to the task. Linet (like most of the court) was unaware of Gareth's true identity and knew him only as Beaumains, a lowly kitchen knave. Linet was furious and left the court immediately. Gareth raced after her, determined to prove himself both to her and the rest of the court. Despite her constant insults, Gareth remained courteous. While passing through the Perilous Passage, he valiantly overcame the Black Knight, the Blue Knight, and the Green Knight, but still Linet withheld her approval and kindness.

A cruel and dreadful sight met them as they approached Castle Perilous. There in the trees hung the bodies of 40 knights; the brave and noble men who had come before. All could be identified by their shields that hung about their necks.

"This is the work of the Red Knight," said Linet, "but now you must turn your thoughts to courage or you shall suffer the same fate."

Gareth then dismounted and blew the ivory horn which hung from a tree, issuing a challenge to the Red Knight of the Red Launde.

A confident Ironside emerged from his red pavilion. "Be aware, young man, of the knights who hang in the trees."

"You are wrong to think this fears me," replied Gareth, "as it gives me courage and strength to put an end to your wicked custom."

The battle began in the morning and by evening both were weak, unable even to stand. As they rested, Gareth could see Lyones cry as she watched from her window. She felt Gareth's eyes upon her and made a deep curtsy. At this, Gareth felt his heart leap. With renewed vigour he began the battle again and would end it in triumph.

Ironside cried for mercy, explaining that his terrible deeds had been done at the bidding of the woman he loved. This woman believed her brother to have been killed by Lancelot or Gawain, and Ironside had understood that if he were to win her love he must take revenge against them, and all of the Knights of the Round Table.

On learning this, Gareth replied, "If the Lady Lyones will forgive you, I shall spare your life and send you to the court where you shall be at the mercy of Lancelot and my brother Gawain."

And so it was that Ironside had much to repent, but was spared and pledged allegiance to Arthur.

13. DEATH

RULED BY SCORPIO

13 DEATH

GWYN AB NUDD
& THE WILD HUNT

GWYN AB NUDD
& THE WILD HUNT

MEANING

Death and rebirth. Transformation. The illusion of death, separating the self from the past in order to start anew. The end of an era or relationship.

A major and necessary change in lifestyle, giving a sense of freedom and renewal. A sudden and involuntary change raises fears of the unknown, but ultimately stimulates growth and generally heralds the dawn of a positive cycle.

Fear of loss. Can mean death or the fear of death. The natural course of events.

REVERSED

Old habits hinder growth. Feeling held back, stifled, and yet unwilling to risk change. This adds to the burden, and leads to an enforced traumatic change. Avoiding the inevitable brings boredom and depression.

DESCRIPTION AND SYMBOLISM

Storm clouds breathe form to Gwyn ab Nudd and his Wild Hunt. The castle ruins represent the end of an era. Its destruction forces growth and a change of lifestyle more appropriate to current needs.

Gwyn ab Nudd was believed by some to have mastered the weather. In harnessing its force he commands the winds of change. In hiding from necessary change one often tempts the hand of fate which can make for a sudden jolt and thorough sweep, as symbolized by the lightning.

Gwyn carries a horn which he blows to rally his shadowy troop. This represents the warning sign of what approaches. Those who feel the air can sense the unrest of an oncoming storm and take measures to prepare themselves.

The leafless tree speaks of the season—the darktime, the reign of Gwyn ab Nudd. The passage through the time of shadows brings insight, heightened psychic abilities, and depth. The veil between this world and the next is thin; it is the dark before the dawn.

No matter if prince or pauper, death is the great leveller, as symbolized by the skeletons which are all equal; one and the same.

Water has traditionally divided this world from the realm of the dead. The Celts believed the sea or a river (much like Styx) ran between the two. Water has long been regarded as a source of life, representing beginnings. The river, like life, must follow its natural course and join the sea.

GWYN AB NUDD
& THE WILD HUNT

wyn, son of Nudd, is the Welsh Wild Huntsman, God of the Dead. Hunter and warrior, he is Lord of the Underworld. The sight of the Wild Hunt streaking through the sky was believed to fortell a coming death, as Gwyn was assigned the task of collecting the souls of the dead.

His ghostly fleet was said to be made up of men fallen in battle. Some rode horses, others stags, all accompanied by the red-eared hounds of the Otherworld (cwn Wyhir).

The riders of the Wild Hunt were also charged with protecting the dead. With thundering hooves and deafening horns their violent passage through the skies was said to scare evil away from the realm of Annwn.

Glastonbury was reputed to be the home of Gwyn, housing him and his spectral host within its hollow hill. It was said that one could access the Otherworld by way of this tor.

According to the *Anglo-Saxon Chronicle*, Arthur accompanies Gwyn on his wild hunt. They also cross paths in the story of Creiddylad. Gwyn is in love with Creiddylad. Despite his affection, arrangements have been made for her to marry Gwythr, son of Gwreidawl. Desperate to prevent the marriage, Gwyn abducts the fair Creiddylad. Arthur pursues Gwyn and lays siege to his fortress. He insists that Creiddylad be released, but Gwyn fails to yield to Arthur's demands. Eventually, it is agreed that Gwyn and Gwythr will fight for the hand of Creiddylad. The battle will take place on May Day, and it is decreed that it shall be repeated every May Day till the end of time. Then, whomever is the victor shall win the fair Creiddylad.

It has been suggested that this annual struggle is symbolic of winter and summer's custody battle for the land.

14. TEMPERANCE
RULED BY SAGITTARIUS

THE CAULDRON OF ANNWN

MEANING

Moderation, patience, and diplomacy. Consistent behaviour. Successfully mixing two different attributes of the personality. The balance of passion and reason guards against extremes.

The art of bridging the spiritual and mundane worlds. The visionary tempered with self-discipline is able to communicate ideas and better cope with life. The synchronized conscious and subconscious enable psychic insights to be applied to physical life, bringing a sense of harmony and progress.

Successful management of a multifaceted endeavour. Clairvoyance and visionary art.

REVERSED

Living an unbalanced lifestyle. Being deaf to the inner voice. Inability to resolve a clash of ideas. Rigidity stifles imagination, leading to the appearance of a barren life. Hostility and difficulty working with others.

DESCRIPTION AND SYMBOLISM

Nine priestesses attend the Cauldron of Annwn, source of poetic inspiration and mantic powers. Many peoples have attributed the powers of prophecy, inspiration, and art to magical springs, cauldrons, and heads. All three motifs have been incorporated into the scene, representing the collective unconscious wisdom available to one who seeks it.

The bards of Arthur's time credited their talents to the Cauldron of Annwn, which originally was thought to have been a head. This echoes the card's alternative name, Art, since it is the arts that most often achieve and communicate knowledge of the unearthly.

One priestess holds a torch, its fire representing the conscious mind and structure. Another of the priestesses pours water, representing the subconscious and the genius of inspiration. It was the custom to mix wine with water and this mixing symbolizes moderation, the combining and balancing of both the physical and spiritual plane. The priestess has one leg in the water while the other rests on the stone. She bridges both worlds, representing one who is capable of manifesting psychic knowledge on this plane.

The sisterhood of nine priestesses combines energies, forming a union of forces which illustrates the value of compatibility, diplomacy, and accommodation.

THE CAULDRON OF ANNWN

Despite Arthur's impressive career, in the early days he felt rivalry with the former legendary King of the Isle of the Mighty, Bran the Blessed. Bran had given the gift of a magical Cauldron of Rebirth to the Irish. It was believed that if the bodies of fallen soldiers were placed in the cauldron their lives would be restored, though not their ability to speak. Bran would come to regret his generosity as it would lead to undue hardships for his people in the battles that followed.

The young and rather impulsive Arthur decided that the best way to eclipse the exploits of the much-loved Bran would be to win the mysterious Cauldron of Annwn for the people of Britain. This Otherworldly cauldron was known to be the source of poetic inspiration and prophetic knowledge. As a Cauldron of Plenty it also sustained its people, but would not cook food for a coward.

The quest for the magical cauldron is a favoured theme amongst the myths of the Celts. *The Book of Taliesin* contains a wonderful poem telling of the quest for the Cauldron of Annwn, known as "The Spoils of Annwfn." Because of similarities in the two tales, it is considered by some to be the model for the later Quest for the Holy Grail.

Three ships carried Arthur and his party from the shores of Britain in search of the Land of the Faery and its treasure.

Accompanying Arthur aboard Pridwen was a reluctant bard. Having had dealings with the Old Ones in the past, Taliesin was well aware of the dangers of entering the Twilight Land. Not only were they uninvited, but they planned to do battle and raid the stores of the Fay. Such a journey was sure to bring misery and despair. Taliesin warned that no venture could be more fraught with peril, but despite this Arthur and company pressed on.

The seas carried them to the destined land where uncharted isles loomed in the soft glow of twilight. The company weaved through the islands, passing seven fortresses before reaching the revolving glass Castle of the Cauldron. Here the Forever Young mixed their sparkling wine and awaited the daring mortals. We do not fully understand the battle and events that followed. Taliesin's account is much like the mysterious land itself, only gently illuminated by twilight, still guarding many secrets.

One certainty is that the battle was dreadful beyond words. It would be the first and only time the king's army would battle the Fay.

Arthur did eventually reach the Cauldron of Annwn. It was described as dark blue, rimmed with pearls, and kindled by the breath of nine maidens with a spring flowing beneath it. 'Twas a scene of great beauty.

A later version of the tale asserts that when Arthur grasped the Cauldron he found he could not move it, nor release his grip. The Faery then captured him and threw him into the Prison of the Strange-Very Strange. This structure was made entirely of mortal bones with innumerable little cells built into its walls; none could escape this labyrinth. The prison held three other men of royal blood—three kings who had offended the Faery and now were doomed, as were their lands, to suffer for eternity. Arthur languished here for three days and three nights, all the while in great agony, his mind curdled by the power of the Fay. It was Llwch Lleminawc and Bedivere who rescued their sovereign, breaking in the roof and returning him to Pridwen. Despite being back with his men, Arthur did not speak for a day and a night and then only wept.

Though they had succeeded in stealing the Cauldron it could hardly have been called a victory, as only seven men returned to Britain when three ships had sailed.

The king did recover his wits and from then on forbade anyone to speak of the raid on Annwn.

15. THE HORNED ONE
RULED BY CAPRICORN

CERNUNNOS

MEANING

The oppression of an unhealthy situation revives the primordial nature of one's self. How this energy is used determines the positive or negative interpretation of the card. When channelled it can empower, motivating courageous and liberating feats. These animal instincts can also serve to protect us; an internal alarm system warning against danger. Though an encounter with the shadow is enlightening, its awesome seductive power can be overwhelming, leading to a disorienting experience. If the primitive, instinctive nature is not integrated but allowed to rule, behaviour becomes reckless, and at times self-destructive. This leads to the more traditional interpretation of the card: violence, controlling relationships, promiscuity, and drug abuse.

REVERSED

The dangerous repression of the instinctive nature risks an uncontrolled eruption. Stunted development of the personality. Trying to alleviate suffering through temporary distractions, such as indulging in drugs, food, sex, shopping, etc. An artificial experience of life.

DESCRIPTION AND SYMBOLISM

Cernunnos—Lord and Protector of Beasts—rests in the wilds. In a card reading, it can reflect wild, unconventional behaviour. Because of the likeness, some may think him the devil of Christianity, but here we are concerned with his original ministry—Lord of the Forest.

Cernunnos symbolizes the animal instincts within humans. The zodiac embodies the concept of animal attributes manifested in human behaviour as well as the processes of integration and development.

The animals represent different aspects of primal wisdom. The fox symbolizes intuition and cunning. He is a lightning spirit and the Trickster. The otter represents the transformational, playful nature. The serpent is knowledge and understanding. The boar stands for force, resistance, and overcoming fear. The stag shows proliferation and humanity's relationship with nature. Lastly, the frog represents impulse, fertility, and creativity.

The moonlight, with its illusionary quality, suggests the difficulty of distinguishing the contents of the subconscious. In this borderland the conscious tends to project, making things seem what they are not. This contamination can lead to overwhelming fears, preventing one from recognizing and benefiting from the valuable assets of the shadow.

The woodland represents the wilderness beyond the conscious, the habitat of the Horned One.

CERNUNNOS

he powerful and archaic image of the Horned God dates back to the palaeolithic age. The Lord of the Animals was a nature deity and God of the Hunt. The Celts were a people whose lives were intrinsically woven with the natural world and the animals that surrounded them. Animal gods were especially popular. Since their survival depended on the welfare of the animals they hunted, the Stag God was particularly revered. The success of the hunt depended on his favour, as he governed not only the animals, but also humanity's relationship to nature, ensuring the ecological balance of preservation and harvest of the wild game.

Frightening yet fascinating, the appearance of Cernunnos echoes the threatening yet irresistible power contained in the primordial self. This is a reminder of the challenge we face when encountering our animal impulses. Aggression, mating, and herding instincts are but a few of the traits that reside here. To repress them can create unhealthy, distorted perversions; yet when uninhibited they create chaos. The body of Cernunnos symbolizes the integration and balance—part man, part beast. He retains the primordial wisdom and vitality of the beast and yet has achieved consciousness. This affords him a supernatural power with which he controls and protects the animals. He is their Master, hence the torc, symbol of a chieftain, while the antlers are symbols of his maturity and vitality.

Though Cernunnos has a strong association with the stag (occasionally even riding one), he also appears with other, generally horned animals who suggest masculine strength. The Gundestrup Cauldron (first century BC) depicts Cernunnos attended by the stag, ram-horned snake, bull, and boar. Since the Horned One embodies the masculine principle, he is believed to be the consort of the Goddess—Mother Earth. Their union holds the promise of fertile lands and an adequate source of game.

The potent image of the Horned God continued to hold sway over its people, despite the efforts of the new Christian church to stamp him out. Predictably this rivalry led to the worship of the Horned One being considered blasphemous and an affront to the church. Ultimately the image of the Horned One would be condemned to represent the devil of the Christian religion. Nevertheless, the Horned Hunter has survived in folklore, art, placenames and even Shakespeare as Herne the Hunter in *The Merry Wives of Windsor.* The enduring popularity of Pan attests to the appeal of the pastoral God. Part man, part beast, God of Shepherds and Huntsmen, the roles of Pan and Cernunnos are virtually one and the same.

Our limited understanding of the worship of the Celtic Horned God and Celtic religion in general is due in part to their practice of memorizing their religious teachings rather than committing them to writing, as this was considered sacrilege. In turning to other cultures where ancient customs are better preserved, we gain a glimpse of what it may have been like. The Chief or Shaman of the tribe appears at a sacred rite, destined to bring fertility and an adequate source of game to his people. In animal guise, washed in firelight he dances, imitating the movement and behaviour of the animal. Chants and the rhythm of the drums induce a trance; the human form sinks and the beauty of the animal soul rises. In such a setting the chief is transformed, possessed by his totem animal god.

Nikolai Tolstoy, in his book *Quest for Merlin,* points out that Myrddin (identified with the Merlin of Geoffrey of Monmouth) fulfils this role. Driven mad by his dreadful experience of the battle of Arderydd, the suffering Myrddin retreated to the isolation of the forest. There he foraged with the animals, wore the antlers and skins of the animals, and gained a supernatural control over their behaviour. Here, Merlin is the "Lord of the Animals, The Horned One."

16. THE TOWER
Ruled by Mars

VORTIGERN'S FORTRESS

MEANING

Unheeded warnings; a false sense of security. War and destruction. Revolutionary change and anxiety. The breakdown of a belief system under pressure. No longer being able to deny the truth. The facing of one's fears.

Abandonment and loss of stability in relationships. Questionable trust. Unexpected trauma and financial losses. Destruction of the old paves the way for the new. Revelation, enlightenment, and an opportunity to make a fresh start.

REVERSED

Being trapped in a stale and oppressive lifestyle. Lack of confidence; fear of the unknown and disappointment. The haunting of past failures and the need to control obstructs beneficial change.

DESCRIPTION AND SYMBOLISM

Vortigern's fortress falls. Built as a refuge from invading Saxons, it represents his futile attempts to insulate himself from the consequences of his own actions.

The keep is symbolic of the mind that created it. Under great stress, previously adequate belief systems buckle, represented by the cracks and crumbling of the walls. Flames whip the keep, suggesting the mental anguish associated with sudden change. The scaffold represents the efforts of the intellect to contain and deal with the upheaval. As can be seen, its effect is minimal. This is an irrepressible transformation.

Intolerable pressure has awakened primal forces. This is symbolized by the two dragons who rise up from their resting place—a pool of water deep within the earth. This is a direct experience with elemental power. The ground ruptures and gives way, shaking the foundations of one's life.

The lightning carries a message on two levels. As the long arm of fate, it echoes the futility of trying to hide from inevitable change, while it also symbolizes revelation in the form of a sudden jolt and blinding flash, putting an end to outmoded thinking.

The scorched land now unencumbered gives way to new life—the eternal cycle of destruction and creation.

VORTIGERN'S FORTRESS

ne of the stories of the Welsh *Mabinogion* tells us that long ago, many years before the time of Arthur, the King of Britain was a man named Lludd. He was a fine warrior, generous and kind. Britain prospered under his reign, with the exception of three plagues. One of these plagues was a terrible scream heard every May Eve throughout the realm. It was so chilling a sound that it caused people to lose their senses and stripped the land of her fruits.

Llefelys, brother of Lludd, told the king that the only way to rid the people of this horror was to find the center of the land, dig down into the earth, and there he would find two fighting dragons, the source of the scream. These dragons would then have to be subdued with the finest mead, and once asleep, transported and hidden, buried deep beneath the earth in the strongest place in the land. Lludd did all Llefelys had instructed and buried the sleeping dragons in Snowdonia in a strong place that would come to be known as Dinas Emrys. Just as his brother had assured, the land was left in peace.

Five hundred years passed and again the people of the land lived in terror. Vortigern, the usurper, sat upon the throne. He had hired Saxon mercenaries to drive back the northern raiders, but the Saxons took a liking to the lush lands of Britain and thought to claim it for themselves. Vortigern had opened the door to invaders.

He took refuge in Wales. There, under the council of his magi, he prepared to build a fortress on what seemed a fitting spot—Dinas Emrys.

The labour of Vortigern's men proved to be in vain, as each morning they found their achievements of the preceding day in ruins. The fortress would not stand. The confounded Vortigern turned to his magi who then advised him to sacrifice a fatherless boy and sprinkle his blood upon the foundations; only then would the structure hold.

Vortigern's men found such a boy in south Wales. He and his mother were then brought before the king at Dinas Emrys. The boy told Vortigern that his name was Ambrosius (or Merlin, according to Geoffrey of Monmouth's account). Sensing the nature of Vortigern's plans, the young Ambrosius/Merlin dared to confront the druids, asking if they knew the reason for the nightly destruction. Having confessed to their ignorance, Merlin turned to face Vortigern, explaining that if he were to dig down beneath the site he would reach a pool of water which had undermined his fortress; within the pool he would find two dragons, one red, the other white. This was done, and once the dragons were unearthed they began to fight.

Merlin spoke, blaming the destruction of the fortress on the fierce nocturnal battles of the dragons. Vortigern was clearly impressed with the talents of the youth. But Merlin had more yet to say. Turning his gaze to the battling dragons, he told all present that the red dragon represented the Britons while the white represented the Saxons. The crowd looked on the symbolic battle in horror as the white dragon seemed to overpower the defending red dragon. Merlin prophesied that the rivers of the land would run red with blood before Britain recovered and drove back the Saxon tide. But Vortigern would not be the king to lead his country to victory. Merlin foretold that Vortigern's life would be taken by either the Saxons, Aurelius Ambrosius, or Uther. Vortigern's enemies were many— his end was near.

17. THE STAR
RULED BY AQUARIUS

17 THE STAR

THE FIREDRAKE

THE FIREDRAKE

MEANING

Hope; a good omen and inspiration. Rebirth and opportunity. Rejuvenation of the spirit after a trying and traumatic time. Freedom and a clear head allows a broader vision of the future. A chance to take a deep breath, contemplate, and draw inspiration from the natural beauty that surrounds you.

Recognizing and believing in the future. Wholeness and healing. The calm allows one to connect with the soul. Destined aspirations now seem to flow naturally into reality. Faith brings strength and peace. Recognition. A welcomed leader. Openness and a free flow of energy.

REVERSED

Pessimism and doubt. Fear keeps you from recognizing possibilities. Not looking at the whole picture. Being uptight and unable to appreciate or benefit from signs of hope. The end of an unfulfilling situation, partnership, or project.

DESCRIPTION AND SYMBOLISM

The dragon of comets heralds the promise of a new era. The storm clouds of the Tower have passed, followed by clear skies indicating calm, fresh air, and a chance to regroup. In this peace one can recognize good omens sent from above.

The comet blazes through the heavens and the hearts of people. The star was thought to be a divine messenger; the call of destiny instills great hope and faith in brighter days to come. The smaller stars represent aspirations and the coming of the comet encourages one to take heart and reach for them.

The horsemen ride in an open landscape, reflecting the freedom associated with the card. The winds blow cobwebs from the mind, clearing it of complicated details and deadwood. Now we are able to recognize the broader scope of things. Here the horsemen break from their journey, water the horses, and marvel at the sight. This symbolizes that one can be content to rest and contemplate at this point in time.

One of the horsemen draws water from the lake; this represents tapping into a free-flowing source of energy. The water is the source of life; it purifies and heals the weary.

With this rejuvenation and new clarity of vision one can appreciate and draw both strength and inspiration from the surrounding beauty—hence, the fireflies in the foreground: hearts are warmed by the sight of little beacons in the night.

THE FIREDRAKE

I n the turbulent times preceding Arthur's reign the land was ruled by (according to Geoffrey of Monmouth) Arthur's grandfather, Constantine. On his assassination (he was poisoned by a Pict) the wily Vortigern saw an opportunity to seize the throne.

Constantine had three sons, the oldest of whom was a monk named Constans. Vortigern encouraged Constans to leave his monastery and take up the crown. Constans followed the advice of Vortigern, but not much time passed before he too was assassinated. Vortigern then made his move and took the throne.

Under such dangerous conditions, the guardians of Constantine's two younger sons had the children taken out of the country to Brittany, safe from the ambitions of Vortigern. Residing here was the future hope of Britain—two boys, Aurelius Ambrosius and Uther, later to be the father of Arthur. In the days ahead, the people of Britain would draw strength from whispering their names and rumours of their ultimate return.

While the boys grew, learned the arts of war, and raised an army, the policies of Vortigern plunged Britain into darkness. The Saxon mercenaries he had invited to Britain now entertained thoughts of conquering it for themselves. Despite this threatening undercurrent, Vortigern, drunk and driven by desire, offered Hengist, their leader, the land of Kent in trade for his daughter Rowena. This arrangement had disastrous consequences. The Britons were outraged at having a Saxon queen and her kinsmen set about conquering the surrounding land. It was said that the cruelty of their ways drove the people of Britain ever westward; some may have even left the Isle. Aside from these troubles, "the Council of the Britons" had want of Vortigern as, whether true or not, charges of incest with his daughter now hung over his head.

In light of all this, Vortigern fled to Wales (see the Tower card). It is here, in these dire times, that we see the triumphant return of Ambrosius and Uther. They crossed the channel and led their army into Wales, trapping Vortigern in a fort. The fort caught fire in the battle that followed. The flames put an end to Vortigern and his tyranny.

The brothers then turned their attention to the Saxons and captured Hengist, who was put to death for the murders of British noblemen.
His remaining followers were consequently driven back.

Britain began a slow recovery under the wise rule of Ambrosius. At
the news of his death by poison, the people, still suffering from their traumatic past, braced themselves and gingerly looked for favourable signs of
the future. It is during this precarious time that a beautiful comet traced
the skies above the Isle of the Mighty. Its unusual shape resembled a
dragon, which led Merlin to proclaim that it portended to Uther the Pendragon ("Head Dragon") the success of his coming reign, and his son who
would unite and bring peace to the land. Uther also drew inspiration from
the omen and gave instructions to have two dragons fashioned of gold,
one of which would become his battle standard. Uther would then come
to be known as the Pendragon—the name, title, and standard that he
would later pass on to his son.

18. THE MOON
RULED BY PISCES

MORGAN LE FAY

MEANING

Unconscious activity, emotions, illusion, and bewilderment. A period of emotionally charged dreams, which have a strong influence on one's waking life. An active imagination floods the conscious mind with enigmatic images which can be both frightening and peaceful and thus disorienting.

A period of introspection. Obscurity, searching, and personality complexes. A need to guard against influence and deception. The struggle to distinguish between reality and illusion. Sensitivity to mythological undercurrents.

The combined energies of intuition, imagination, and intellect bring great wisdom.

REVERSED

Errors in judgement. Repressed unconscious issues causing mood swings and affecting one's health. Feeling edgy and impatient. Suppressing the intuitive sense. Avoiding one's own thoughts through hyperactivity—a practice which only feeds fears, and can lead to paranoia and hysteria.

DESCRIPTION AND SYMBOLISM

Fostered by the magic of the moon, Morgan travels the threshold of uncharted worlds. The moon governs the waxing and waning of emotions and energy levels. Her association with the subconscious represents limitless inspiration for the imagination. Reflecting the conscious light of the sun, the moon illuminates the hidden realms of the mind. Emotions, intuition, and dreams bring to light issues and ideas of which we were previously only vaguely aware. The pool symbolizes the expansive knowledge contained in the subconscious. The reflections on the surface represent the difficulty of understanding the significance of its calling, as it is often distorted through imperfect methods of communication. The light of the moon alters both the physical and the mental landscape. What was comfortable in the light of day becomes menacing under the light of the moon. Travelling this realm can be a harrowing experience, promoting a chaotic, lawless imagination. This reminds us of the belief that the moon could cause one to lose his or her wits; a belief reflected in such words as *lunacy, lunatic, moonstruck,* and the somewhat gentler term, *moon-kissed.* The raven patiently sits in the branches of the tree, a sinister reminder of these dangers, while the tree itself symbolizes the involuntary psychic growth attained through this phase.

MORGAN LE FAY

he famed Morgan le Fay is the beautiful, intelligent, and talented female counterpart to the magician Merlin. There is no doubt that the portrait of Morgan the Goddess is of great antiquity. More than eight centuries have passed since her literary debut in *Vita Merlin*, and yet Morgan continues to fascinate and inspire modern works. Her divine origins can be traced through early Welsh genealogy. Under the name Modron, her father is Avallach and her grandfather the God Beli. Morgan is also associated with the Gaulish goddess Matrona and the Irish Morrigan ("great queen"), goddess of war and death.

Morgan reinforces the feminine principle of the Moon card; as enchantress she draws on its lunar power. Having prepared herself, she accepts its disturbing influence, experiencing it as enriching rather than frightening. Morgan neither resists nor obsesses over the moon's expression and influence. She is a calm spectator of the fantastic displays of illusion and insight. In league with the moon, she benefits from sharpened intuition and psychic abilities which aid her when she returns to her journey and the blinding light of day.

A winterless isle was said to be the home of Morgan and her sisterhood of nine. Here they studied, among other subjects, medicine and the magical arts. Morgan was particularly revered for her healing talents. Under the influence of medieval Christianity, Morgan's historical character became debased. Sensitive to her obvious Pagan origins and feminine power, she is stripped of her divinity and left simply as Arthur's half sister, a meddling witch. As history has demonstrated, the witch often becomes the scapegoat, and so Morgan is made to carry the blame for the troubles of the land.

In the romances, Morgan takes every opportunity to provoke Arthur. She steals Excalibur, gives him the gift of a cloak that burns, and busies herself devising some humorous means of exposing Guenevere's affair. Morgan involved the unsuspecting Tristram in one of her plots, sending him to one of the king's tournaments bearing a shield which depicted the king and queen with Lancelot standing atop their heads. In another attempt to expose Guenevere, she sent a magical drinking horn to the court. Only a faithful woman could drink from the horn without spilling its contents. Whether Morgan is portrayed in a positive or negative light, she consistently maintains an air of mystery. Even when on friendly terms with her brother and staying at his court, she would often disappear into the night, preferring her own company and the moonlit woods to the activity of the court.

19. THE SUN
Ruled by the Sun

LLEU

MEANING

Joy, light, and energy. Clarity of vision. Optimism and success. An understanding of the heart's true desires. An appreciation of the beauty and simplicity of life. Knowledge, wholeness, and strength. A feeling of value and purpose.

Artistic achievement or the completion of an unusual project. Good health, friendship, and activity. Safety and security, allowing one to enjoy the pleasures of time in the sun.

Commitment; a happy marriage. A breakthrough. Well-deserved acclaim enthusiastically celebrated with friends.

REVERSED

Confusion and suspicion prevent one from enjoying the warmth of the sun. Entertaining fantasies of success unsupported by a realistic plan for achievement. Broken promises; the crumbling of an alliance. The possibility of partial happiness if one makes an effort to appreciate what rays of sun break through the clouds.

DESCRIPTION AND SYMBOLISM

The increasing strength of the rising sun lends its warmth to Lleu. The sun represents the conscious mind, in contrast to the subconscious realm of the moon. Its light symbolizes directed thoughts that bring comfort, plans, and achievements, just as the sun's rays bring warmth, growth, and the harvest.

Lleu is the Welsh counterpart to the Irish God Lug. Here, he represents the bright blessings of the sun; with the power of its light and his own talents he brings order out of the moon's disorienting power. The presence of Lleu also emphasizes the quality of commitment. Lleu was the deity evoked to preside over the sacred marriage between the king and the land, a connection upon which the welfare of all depended. The invincible sword of Lleu symbolizes the discriminating power of the intellect and its ability to cut away outmoded and incongruent behaviour or thought patterns. This is reinforced by his cloak of red, the colour of Lleu (and later of Galahad), symbolic of passionate dedication manifested in worldly activity. The horse is a symbol of progress and wisdom. The Faery horses of the heroes were able to cover great distances in short periods of time. Often these Otherworldly horses were able to speak, passing on valuable knowledge to their riders.

LLEU

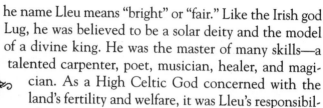

he name Lleu means "bright" or "fair." Like the Irish god Lug, he was believed to be a solar deity and the model of a divine king. He was the master of many skills—a talented carpenter, poet, musician, healer, and magician. As a High Celtic God concerned with the land's fertility and welfare, it was Lleu's responsibility to oversee the sacred marriage between land and king. Building on the tradition established by Lleu, it is supposed that the coronation ritual of a king involved a druid-seer who prophesied the coming succession of kings. In this context the words of the soothsayer were thought to be the words of Lleu and it is clear how Lleu's poetry and prophecy were held to bring peace and harmony out of chaos.

The festival of Lleu or Lug is known as Lughnasa, occurring on the first day of August. This celebration would take place amidst standing stones. Aside from the relevant rituals, there would be horse races, plays, dancing, and games, all of which took on a religious significance. The design of prehistoric Avebury Ring, which stands not far from Stonehenge in the south of England, has led some to speculate that it was a solar temple. In the magical tradition the circle affords protection, while the standing stones of mystical centres are thought to tap a higher energy. Thus Avebury Ring is a magic circle on the grandest scale, representing the energizing and protective qualities of the suncard.

A story in the Welsh *Mabinogion* tells of Lleu's mother, Aranrhod, and her desire to serve Math, greatest of magicians. It was said that Math could only walk the land when his country was at war and in need of his aid. The remaining time he was required to sit with his feet in the lap of a virgin, or he would cease to exist. When asked, Aranrhod told Math that she was a virgin, but the magician devised a test for her. As she stepped across Math's magical wand, Aranrhod failed, giving birth to both Lleu and his brother Dylan ("son of the wave"). Angry at being exposed, Aranrhod refused to see her sons and laid three curses on Lleu: first, that he would never have a name unless it be given by her; second, that he would never bear arms unless invested by her; and third, that he would never have a wife of the race that inhabits the earth.

It was Math's nephew, Gwydion, who raised the boy; a child who, because of his connection to solar powers, grew at twice the normal rate. Gwydion managed to trick Aranrhod into naming the child Lleu Llaw Gyffes—"Bright One of the Skillful Hand." He also managed to deceive her into equipping her son with arms. But in the matter of the wife, Gwydion's magic waned and he enlisted the aid of Math. With his supreme arts Math conjured a maiden out of oak, broom, and meadowsweet blossoms. She was given the name Blodeuwedd, meaning "Flower Face." But as beautiful as she was, Blodeuwedd would later betray her husband, taking a lover named Gronw and with his help plotting Lleu's death. Being of divine origin, Lleu was vulnerable only under the most complex and unlikely circumstances. The cunning Blodeuwedd persuaded her husband to confide these deadly details. He must be neither inside nor outside, neither on foot nor horseback. He must stand with one foot in a cauldron that has been used as a bath and is covered with a thatched roof. The other foot must rest on the body of a he-goat; lastly, the spear that inflicts the fatal wound must have been made over a period of one year, and only when folk attend Sunday Mass.

A year passed and Gronw finished the spear, according to the specifications. Blodeuwedd pleaded with her husband to show her the fateful position so she would understand what she must guard against. The trusting Lleu agreed. Gronw hid in the woods awaiting his chance. He threw the spear, but it missed Lleu's head and entered his side. A great scream went up; Lleu transformed into an eagle and disappeared into the sky. Gronw then claimed Lleu's wife and lands for himself. The news travelled to Math and Gwydion who set out in search of the wounded Lleu. A sow eventually led Gwydion to a tree where, high in its branches, the suffering eagle hid. Gwydion sang to the bird, coaxing it from its height, then touched it with his wand, restoring Lleu's shape. Once nursed back to health, he and Gwydion returned to avenge the betrayal. Gronw hid behind a stone, but this was of little use as Lleu's spear travelled through the stone and killed him. Gwydion, meanwhile, had found Blodeuwedd and transformed her into an owl, commanding her to only show her face at night. The owl would thereafter be known as Blodeuwedd—Flower Face.

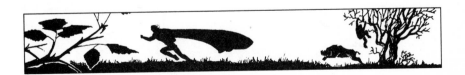

20. THE JUDGEMENT
Ruled by Pluto

AVALON

MEANING

The awakening call of one's destiny. An effort to understand life's higher purpose. New perceptions enhance and expand one's philosophy.

Improvement, development, and change. Reaching a crossroads and conducting a self-evaluation. The acceptance of responsibility. An understanding of how one's actions influence others. A need for fair, responsible conduct. Acclaim, promotion, and reward. The hope that one's deeds and achievements will bring immortality. Good health; a judgement in a legal matter.

REVERSED

Denying the truth of a matter. Procrastination. Exaggerating obstacles which then become convenient excuses for not risking change. Stagnation, divorce, disappointment. Vain attempts to recapture youth. Refusing to accept that reality has changed poses the danger of life passing one by.

DESCRIPTION AND SYMBOLISM

Having travelled through the vales of Avalon, the passing king is brought to rest. This is a rite of passage. Arthur has followed the call and fulfilled his destiny, as symbolized by the water spirit who sounds the Celtic horn. In doing so, she signals the end of one cycle and heralds the arrival of another. Awakened by the blow, spirits stir, and the waves rise up around the vessel and take on the form of undines, indicative of the transformative nature of the card. As reward for his days of campaigning, Arthur is escorted to the Fortunate Isle where he may rest in peace. This journey represents the serving of a judgement that radically alters one's outlook and existence. The isle is hidden by mist, implying that this new existence will remain mysterious until a transformation is undergone and one finally arrives. Only then can one appreciate a land of possibilities. Providing the card is upright, this is change for the better, and brings rewards. As the painting suggests, this course is charted by the winds of fate—one's ship comes in. The four priestesses who accompany Arthur were known to be skilled healers. In the context of the card, they represent a return to good health and support during a transitional period. The body of Arthur represents the passing of the old self. Avalon itself symbolizes the search for youth and immortality associated with the Judgement card. Many people refused to believe Arthur had died, insisting that he remained eternally young on the Isle of Avalon. In a sense, they were correct, as Arthur and his knights have attained immortality through their legendary status and numerous resurrections in modern works.

AVALON

he beautiful Apple Isle was the home of Morgan le Fay and her sisterhood. It has been said that Avalon was the "Fortunate Isle" or the "Isle of the Blessed" which lay in the waters to the west. Glastonbury Tor in Somerset was once surrounded by an "adventurous marsh" and is also reputed to be the Isle of Avalon. There are many claims to this magical place where winter never came, the crops tended themselves, the grass grew only to a manageable height, and the vines always hung heavy with fruit. The nine priestesses of the Isle, particularly their leader, Morgan, were famed healers and shapeshifters. They were learned women whom the people said could control the weather and foretell the future. They pursued all fields of knowledge, but were especially talented in the magical arts. It was believed that Morgan was the Great Goddess incarnate, or at least a vessel through which she worked. Morgan was thus granted great respect and it seems only natural that the dying king be entrusted to her and her company after the fateful battle of Camlann.

As the battle fog lifted, Bedivere held his dying king. Arthur struggled to form words. He ordered his friend to return Excalibur to the water from whence it came. Bedivere was reluctant, not wishing to leave Arthur's side, but agreed to carry out his king's dying wish. He took the sword and rode to the nearest body of water. As he lifted Excalibur and looked a last time on its singular beauty, his heart waned. He could not bring himself to throw away the sacred sword and so hid it beneath a tree. On returning to the king, Arthur asked him what he had seen as he threw the sword. "Nothing but waves and wind," replied Bedivere. At these words the king knew he had lied. Bedivere was sent a second time to return Excalibur to the watery depths, but again he failed. "Would you betray me for the riches of the sword?" asked Arthur. At these harsh words Bedivere did as he was told, throwing Excalibur as far as he could. A hand rose up from the water to meet the sword, grasped it by the hilt, raised it three times, then plunged beneath the surface. Bedivere returned and told the king what he had seen. Arthur then asked his knight to carry him to the water's edge. Waiting in the mists was a barge carrying the priestess Nimue and three queens: the Queen of Northgalis, the Queen of the Wasteland, and the Great Queen Morgan le Fay. Bedivere gently laid his king amongst the four black-hooded figures. With his head upon Morgan's lap, the failing Arthur offered words of comfort to his trusted and noble knight: "Do as thee may and comfort thyself, for I go now into the vale of Avalon to be healed of my wounds." The company then drifted out of sight. Bedivere grieved the loss of his king, gave up his life of arms, and remained in the forest as a hermit the rest of his days. Arthur remained in Avalon from whence, the people say, he and his knights shall return when their country is in need of them.

21. THE UNIVERSE
RULED BY SATURN

THE GIANTS' DANCE

MEANING

Liberation. The attainment of a long-sought goal. The culmination of events, efforts, and experiences from the past. Completing a task with honours. Triumph and prosperity. Winning the admiration of others.

Attainment bringing change that still retains stability. Security and assurance. Synthesis brings a sense of peace and wholeness. May refer to travel, a new home, or graduation. The ability to direct one's life. Confidence, success, and lasting happiness.

REVERSED

Regret. Lingering doubt interferes with decision-making. Delays; lack of support. Losing interest or enthusiasm after beginning a new project. Failing to follow through on plans. Loss of direction; scattered energies.

DESCRIPTION AND SYMBOLISM

Under the heavens and amidst the stones, the dancer celebrates life in her victory dance of being. This ecstasy comes from deep within, when the conscious and subconscious work in unison. This leads to encounters, however brief, with the superconscious and its lasting gifts of faith. This synthesis opens many doors to understanding. The woman's dance represents embracing and enjoying life, living it to its utmost. Her iridescent veil of light drapes about her but does not restrict her movement, representing a flexible lifestyle and environment. She is her perfectly natural, unencumbered self, free to dance in rhythm with the universe. The wand held in her hand symbolizes that she is the mistress of her own fate, not living by the dictates of others. She carries the wand with ease, representing self-confidence and faith; there is no desperate battle for control. As the woman dances she travels the ditch which surrounds the stones. It has been theorized that rituals at these sacred sites involved the king, chief, or druid walking a protective circle, a Path of Blessing. This was thought to harmonize the four energies of the earth, the quaternary powers depicted on the foreground stones. These are the four evangelists traditional to the card, symbolizing the culmination and balance of energies. These figures correspond to the zodiac as: the man/Aquarius, air; the bull/Taurus, earth; the lion/Leo, fire; and the eagle/Scorpio, water. The qualities they bring to the card are, respectively: intelligence and independence; determination and stability; strength and enthusiasm; intuitive knowledge and great spiritual heights. The evangelists in the painting are as they appear in the famous *Book of Kells* (late eighth or early ninth century). The church associates the man with Matthew, Incarnation; the bull with Luke, Passion; the lion with Mark, Resurrection; the eagle with John, Ascension.

THE GIANTS' DANCE

alisbury Plain in the south of England is home to many prehistoric monuments: long barrows, round barrows, Woodhenge, Durrington Walls, and its most famous, Stonehenge. Excavations at the site have revealed that its construction occurred in stages that spanned centuries, from approximately 3100 to 2800 B.C. The earliest structures completed were the ditch, its bank, and the Heel Stone.

The Neolithic people of the time were farmers with small numbers of domesticated animals. Small groups of immigrants, called Beaker People because of their pottery, arrived in eastern and southern Britain sometime after 2500 B.C. They settled and merged with the natives, the two groups becoming a successful community whose efforts likely added to the grandeur of Stonehenge. Construction and remodelling would continue until 1100 B.C. with the extension of the Avenue. Over the centuries, its origins long forgotten, the awesome monument would inspire many tales. As with other stone circles, some of these stories provide food for thought and may carry some truths, while others are fantastic beyond belief. In any event, they are all entertaining.

It has been argued that Stonehenge was once considered the Omphalos, the symbolic "navel" of Britain, the point from which all creation spread and the site where the energies from heaven, earth, and the underworld melded together. This is the stream of life, flowing through the World Tree from its pole star heights to the depths of its roots in the underworld. Thus, the presence of Stonehenge represents an arrival at a point in one's development in which previously fragmented energies unite. This emancipation brings a sense of completion and affords a new lease on life. The circle of stones reminds us of life's circular nature. The Universe card marks the end of the Major Arcana, but with new optimism we find we have come full circle to rest with the hope and vitality of the Fool card. The mystery which hangs about Stonehenge echoes the mysterious quality of the Universe card; it always contains an element of the unknown.

As one might expect, Merlin is associated with the stones. This is quite plausible as a person in his position would surely be familiar with the famous site, whether involved in its construction or not. It was said that Merlin used the temple to track the stars, while Geoffrey of Monmouth went so far as to claim it to be of Merlin's construction.

King Vortigern and his council had been invited by the Saxon leader Hengist to a conference. Hengist claimed he had treaty proposals he wished to discuss. Once the two sides sat down to negotiate, however, the Saxon guards pulled out the daggers they had hidden in their boots and massacred the 460 nobles. They were later buried in a mass grave on Salisbury Plain. Years later, when Ambrosius had restored relative peace to the country, he decided that the victims of the treachery should have a fitting memorial. When his own workmen failed the task, he summoned Merlin. The sage advised Ambrosius that if he wished for a monument that would stand forever he must send for the Giants' Ring, a megalithic ring of stones which stood on Mount Killaraus in Ireland. The stones were said to have healing powers; illness and wounds were cured by water that had washed over the stones. Ambrosius was not entirely convinced, but eventually agreed to the endeavour, sending Merlin, Uther, and his men to Ireland. The massive stones were dismantled, ferried across the waters, and hauled to Salisbury Plain where Merlin would raise them again. It was only because of Merlin's extraordinary arts (engineering skills) that the feat was ever accomplished. Ambrosius was moved beyond words as he stood beneath the towering stones. Three days of ceremonies followed the erection of the monument, and the grateful Ambrosius then crowned Merlin for his achievements. He had indeed given Ambrosius his everlasting monument, as even today the giants still dance on Salisbury Plain.

SPEARS

THE SUIT OF SPEARS

Spears (Wands, Rods, Sceptres, Batons, etc.) represent the workings of the mind; its ideas, intuition, creativity, and development. They denote the mentality influencing future plans and spiritual, artistic endeavours. Spears symbolize the vital inspiration needed to initiate and sustain pioneering efforts.

The elements assigned to the suits can vary somewhat. Personally, I associate air with the fresh nature of Spears and its elusive manner. It embodies the intangible qualities of inspiration, thoughts, and intuition, all of which can be likened to air.

Spears are associated with the season of spring, reflecting fertility and growth.

ACE OF SPEARS

MEANING

Mental activity and spiritual strength. Beginnings. Revelation brings a renewed sense of purpose. Beginning a new venture. Laying foundations for success. A breakthrough. Sensing great potential. A rise in energy levels. Enhanced perception. Making gains by original thinking. Following intuition. The beginning of a promising relationship. Marriage, fertility, and creativity.

REVERSED

Boredom. Lack of enthusiasm. Facing a barren landscape. Short-lived ventures. Stale ideas. A breakdown in communications. Growth stunted by an inhospitable environment.

THE GRAIL LANCE

The Lance of Redemption rests in the sanctity of the inner chamber. The sacred Lance was kept under the care of the Fisher King in his castle, where it appeared in the famous Grail procession.

The Lance had the power to heal, avenge, and bring fertility to the earth. It most likely originates from the Celtic Lance of Redemption, or Spear of Lug (Lleu). It later became associated with the Christian Lance of Longinus and the spear that injured the Fisher King.

Balin, the Knight of Two Swords, entered the castle of the Fisher King in search of a murderous knight. Balin found and killed the villain, whom he later learned was a relative of the Fisher King. Having lost his weapons, Balin raced through the castle trying to escape the enraged king. The unknowing knight entered the inner chamber of the Lance. The awestruck Balin marvelled at its beauty and sanctity. As he gazed, the king burst through the door. In his panic, Balin grabbed the spear and wounded the king through his thigh. With the Dolorous Stroke (as it has come to be known) the castle fell and the land wasted alongside its king, only to be renewed many years later with the success of the Quest for the Holy Grail.

TWO OF SPEARS

MEANING

Executive responsibilities. Proving one's self capable of managing a large project. Exerting authority. Brainstorming, contemplating, and putting forth ideas for consideration. Planning for the future. Courage and maturity. Using all of one's talents to achieve a communal vision. Employing intuitive insights to assist with decision making. A capable leader, and one who is governed by honourable motives.

REVERSED

Dreading the challenges and obstacles of the future. Being unprepared for the task ahead. Avoiding responsibility. Finding one's self devoid of ideas. Encountering obstacles and delays. Pessimism.

BEDIVERE & KAY

Two of Arthur's oldest and trusted friends devise plans for progress. Bedivere (or Bedwyr) was one of the king's earliest companions, who remained a loyal and close confidant to Arthur throughout his reign (see Knight of Spears).

Kay (or Cei) is generally thought of as Arthur's irritable foster brother and seneschal. In early versions he had a quite different reputation, and was known as a courageous, handsome, and courteous warrior.

Arthur gave the two men the heavy responsibility of administering his provinces in Gaul. Bedivere was posted in Normandy, and Kay in Anjou.

THREE OF SPEARS

MEANING

Practical knowledge. Envisioning possibilities. Trade and negotiations. Thorough research before entering into a business transaction. Nurturing a new enterprise. Making firm, educated decisions. Advancing a step closer to a goal. Ingenuity and partnership. Cultivating the early stages of a successful undertaking.

REVERSED

Not knowing how to proceed. Difficulty in taking the first step. Ideas remain up in the air. A need for self-discipline, to research and acquire the foundation of knowledge to safely initiate the endeavour.

THE HORSE FAIR

With an eye for detail, the experienced horseman studies his prospects.

The horse was of great importance to the people of Dark Age Britain, as they relied heavily upon its strength and mobility. The business of horses and their breeding was a significant part of life. The people took great pride in their stables and the horses they produced.

Aside from the prestige, the horse was central to both domestic life and war. Arthur's success at Mount Badon has been attributed, by some, to his resurrection of the cavalry.

Chalk drawings on hillsides and coins depicting the horse attest to the reverence in which it was held. Each stable had a shrine to the equine goddess: Rhiannon to the British and Epona to the Gauls. These shrines were lovingly adorned with roses to show appreciation for the gift of the horse, and to ensure the continued favour of the deity.

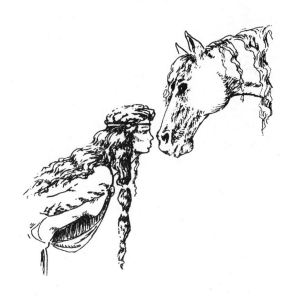

FOUR OF SPEARS

MEANING

Prosperity. Celebrations. Romance and social events. Past efforts come to fruition, bringing great satisfaction. Sharing one's good fortune with others. Creating a secure foundation for the future. Diligent hard work is rewarded with a time of peace. Overcoming obstacles. Emotional and material blessings.

REVERSED

Delayed satisfaction. Lack of recognizable progress. An empty romance. Snobbery. Continued turbulence leaves one feeling insecure, worrying about the lack of material gain.

LA COTE MALE TAIL
& MALEDISANT

The court celebrates the wedding of La Cote Male Tail and the damsel Maledisant.

As a young man Breunor had come to Arthur's court, hoping to become a Knight of the Round Table. He wore an ill-made coat, and because of this was nicknamed "La Cote Male Tail" by Sir Kay.

La Cote Male Tail hoped to prove himself by accepting the Adventure of the Black Shield. This was the most dangerous undertaking of the time, and to make matters worse, the young knight had to endure the cruel tongue of his lady guide, aptly named Maledisant.

Despite La Cote Male Tail's heroics, the damsel rebuked him at every turn. Maledisant later regretted this, as during the course of the adventure she fell in love with the champion. Victorious in his trial, La Cote Male Tail was made a Knight of the Round Table. He then married the damsel Maledisant, whose name was changed to Beauvivante, reflecting her new demeanour. Lancelot, friend and mentor to La Cote Male Tail (as he continued to be called), gave the newlyweds the Castle Pendragon and surrounding lands.

FIVE OF SPEARS

MEANING

Strong competition makes for a lengthy struggle. A breakdown of command under stress. Engaging a challenge offered by staunch opposition. Disorganized effort. Mass confusion. Unfulfilled desires fuel upheaval and conflict. Dedication to a cause. Learning from past mistakes. Reassessing methods and planning a new approach. A need to calmly focus and redirect scattered energies toward one goal.

REVERSED

Being taken in by the trickery of an imposter. Arriving at a dead end. Being misinformed and led astray. Allowing one's self to be deterred by the failure of a first attempt.

PURSUIT OF IGRAINE

The king's men regard the challenge of Tintagel.

Driven by his desire for Igraine, the Duchess of Cornwall, Uther Pendragon led his army against the duke. The duke, in his wisdom, placed Igraine in the Castle of Tintagel, while he and his men awaited Uther in a nearby encampment.

Though they were greatly outnumbered, the duke's men put up a valiant fight, but they were not the only obstacle to face the High King. The greater challenge came from Tintagel itself.

Situated on the rugged coast of Cornwall, Tintagel is surrounded by the sea on three sides. Only a narrow ridge connects its island to the mainland. An added deterrent are its formidable cliffs, which drop up to a hundred meters to the sea. With such defenses the castle only need be guarded by a small garrison of men. (Excavations of the site have revealed that it was inhabited in the fifth and sixth centuries, but the ruins seen today are of the twelfth century.)

A frustrated Uther was advised that it would not matter if the entire kingdom stood behind him, he still would not be able to take Tintagel. Uther realized that if he were to succeed he must abandon his old tactics and take a different approach. For this new approach, the implacable Uther turned to Merlin (see the Magician).

SIX OF SPEARS

SIX OF SPEARS

THE RETURN
OF AMBROSIUS

MEANING

A well-earned victory. Accolades. Reaching a milestone. Commitment to change for the better. Passing through a gateway to a new era. Resolution of a problem. Gaining control of a worrisome situation. Success through hard work and careful planning brings great satisfaction. Out manoeuvreing the opposition. Conquest and advancement. Honours and a warm reception from others. Having a supportive, enthusiastic following.

REVERSED

Apprehension. Worrying over the opposition's agenda. Lack of notable progress lowers morale. Setbacks and delays. Inconclusive results. Unrecognized efforts.

THE RETURN OF AMBROSIUS

Glad hearts rejoice at the victory of Ambrosius.

Amidst the chaos following the death of Constantine, his two young sons, Ambrosius and Uther, were taken and safely hidden in Brittany. During their absence, the people of Britain endured many hardships under the reign of Vortigern, and suffered further under the force of the invading Saxons.

Aurelius Ambrosius matured into a fine, honourable man with many talents. Over the years he and Uther trained an army, and then prepared to reclaim their kingdom.

Merlin prophesied the return of the sons of Constantine, instilling great hope in the people of the land. Once Ambrosius landed upon the British shore, the people rallied around their rightful king.

First on the brothers' agenda was to rid Britain of the tyrant King Vortigern. Having done this, Ambrosius led his forces against the Saxons and their allies.

Though it took a great effort, they eventually were able to subdue the Saxon host.

Aurelius Ambrosius had led his fellow countrymen to their first substantial victory over the invaders, and set the stage for the following triumphs of Arthur.

SEVEN OF SPEARS

MEANING

Overcoming adversity. Gaining recognition and the confidence of others. Surmounting obstacles.

Promoting unity and encouraging all sides to work together for the common good. Defending and nurturing a broad and noble vision. Protecting new and fragile growth. Sustaining the effort needed to realize one's goals. Courage, strength, and success.

REVERSED

Losing faith. Shrinking under the onslaught of steadfast opponents. The negative attitudes of others eat away at one's hopes, creating self-doubt and causing a retreat. A need for one to take heart and stand one's ground.

ARCH OF TWELVE KINGS

The monument of twelve kings stands in testament to the tenacity of Arthur.

The early days of Arthur's reign were tempestuous times. The lesser kings fought bitterly amongst themselves, rather than making a serious effort to abate the tide of invaders. Some of Arthur's policies added to the discontent, and at times rightly so.

The angered nobility often blamed Merlin for the king's misguided actions. Those of the ruling class who desired the kingdom for themselves revelled in his unpopular decisions, and did their utmost to fuel the unrest.

Intent on toppling the young Arthur, twelve rebel kings joined forces and led their host against him. Despite the great strain of civil war, the High King prevailed through this precarious time. As a token of this victory, Merlin crafted twelve figures of copper and brass in the likeness of his subdued opponents. He then made a figure of Arthur to stand over them in triumph. All were gilded in gold, and tapers placed in the hands of the rebel kings. The tapers burnt throughout the day and night, until Merlin's earthy life came to an end and the enchantment was broken.

EIGHT OF SPEARS

MEANING

Excitement. A rapidly approaching opportunity to prove one's self. Progress. Events unfolding at great speed. A good omen; a harbinger.

The beginning of an adventure which tests one's limits. Quick thinking; decisions made in haste.

Travels, wanderlust, and possible advancement. A journey or experience which entails a spiritual lesson.

REVERSED

Getting "carried away" amidst excitement. Rushing into a relationship. Not thinking of the consequences of one's actions. Short-lived pleasures. Conflicts. Setting out on the right path but losing one's way.

THE WHITE HART

The white hart races through the kingdom, leaving chaos in its wake.

The white hart was believed to be a messenger of the gods. Matters of great importance were thought to follow a sighting of the graceful creature.

On the wedding day of Arthur and Guenevere, the all-knowing Merlin insisted that all of the knights remain in their seats for the duration of the feast. Without warning, a white hart raced through the hall, pursued by a brachet and a company of hounds. Chaos erupted within the room. Amidst all the excitement a knight grabbed the brachet and stole it away from the court. As the knight disappeared, a young woman upon a winded horse entered the hall, and cried out for the return of her dog. As the bewildered crowd looked on, a strange knight rode in, grabbed the damsel, and made off with her.

The inexplicable events stunned the crowd, who then looked to Merlin. The sage singled out Gawain, Tors, and Pellinore. He told all present that this was a test, and if the court were to retain its honour the three knights must seek out and return to the court the hart, the brachet and the knight who stole it, and the woman and her abductor.

And so began the Quest of the White Hart (see the Five of Swords).

NINE OF SPEARS

MEANING

Anticipating hostility. Preparing for upheaval and conflict. Foresight. Gaining an advantage by putting one's affairs in order before trouble strikes. The teachings of the past leave one better equipped to cope with hostility. Sensing unrest. Putting up a strong defense. Outwitting an adversary.

REVERSED

Unheeded warnings. Hardship and quarrels. Confusion. Being caught off guard. Difficulty adapting to changing circumstances. Avoidable losses.

WIND HARPS OF WAR

In anticipation of war, giant wind harps are erected upon the cliffs, where their sinister strains will greet the enemy.

The Dark Ages were precarious times for the inhabitants of Britain. They contended with raids, looting, and invasions. All sides faced violence and adversity with only brief periods of relative calm. The ever-present threat meant the labours of war continued through the pages of peace. One could not afford to meet the enemy unprepared, and many hours were spent honing battle skills, fortifying important sites, and crafting weapons. Even those not active on the battlefield were made to contribute by sustaining the warbands that protected them.

The card depicts a weapon of a different sort—one used on the battlefield of the mind. These great harps gave voice to the guardian spirits of the land. The wind whipped against their strings, generating sinister howls and deafening moans that would chill the blood of the bravest enemy. The eerie giants and their foreboding song were a potent weapon of psychological warfare.

TEN OF SPEARS

MEANING

Feeling tremendous pressure. Encountering an awesome task which tests courage and diplomacy. Feeling out of one's depth. Living under the restrictions of a specific code of conduct. Temporarily suppressing personal desires in order to complete a task. Playing by the rules of the game. Striving to please others. Success through perseverance.

REVERSED

Self-defeat. Learning the hard way that there are no short cuts to success. Being distracted by and succumbing to temptation. Walking into a trap.

THE GREEN KNIGHT

The Green Knight scrutinizes the brave Gawain.

As Arthur's court celebrated the Christmas season an unexpected visitor burst into the hall. The horse and rider were larger than life, and both were of a green hue. The knight was richly clad and carried a bough of holly in one hand, and an axe in the other. He issued a challenge to the assembly for one to join him in a game of the season—the Beheading Game. Being that the stranger and his steed gave off a green light, the knights feared him to be of the Faery. Naturally, they were reluctant to meet his challenge.

Gawain was the one to step forward and take up the dare. The Green Knight dismounted, knelt, and explained to Gawain that he would be given one chance to behead him; if he survived, a year later the Green Knight would return the blow.

Gawain struck off the head of the Green Knight, but to his dismay the body stood up, retrieved the head, and placed it back on his shoulders. The knight reminded Gawain that they would meet again in one year. Then, in high humour, he left the court.

During the following year Gawain's honour and fortitude were tested by the Faery cohorts of the Green Knight.

Gawain fared reasonably well, but only just resisted the seductive powers of a beautiful woman (whom he later learned was the wife of the Green Knight). The charming Fay offered Gawain her green garter as a talisman. Gawain accepted the garter, but far from protecting him, the gesture put his life in peril.

When the fateful day came, the Green Knight made his judgement. Being that Gawain's only weakness was enlisting the help of the lady, the knight only nicked Gawain's neck with the axe. Gawain was now free to return to the court, but the Green Knight declared from that day forward he must wear the garter as a token of his fault.

Afterward, as a demonstration of their solidarity, all Knights of the Round Table wore a green garter.

THE PAGE OF SPEARS

MEANING

Stimulating communications. The arrival of good things. Intellectual development and interaction with society. A trustworthy, enthusiastic assistant. A playful, good-humoured friend. An excitable, positive supporter who leads cheers of approval. One who is sincerely pleased to bring news of good fortune.

REVERSED

One who cannot be trusted with confidential matters. Indecision and lack of communication. Warranted suspicion. An immature person with little concern for others. Gossip.

THE HARE

The hare is a totem transformational animal. While it retains some of the attributes of the Trickster, such as the playful comedic nature, it has advanced beyond the selfish manner of the primitive Trickster phase. The hare represents the stage of intellectual development in which the child becomes conscious of the repercussions of its actions upon the outside world. The hare is a social creature, symbolizing an awakening cultural sense and enjoyable interaction with the community.

THE KNIGHT OF SPEARS

MEANING

An attractive, sociable young man, committed to developing his abilities to their full potential. He is intelligent and magnetic. His strategies are generally unpredictable and effective.

A journey or change of residence. Can represent acting on intuition and having the courage to risk unconventional ideas.

REVERSED

One who revels in conflict. Unproductive behaviour. Lack of focus. One who sows discord for entertainment. The breakup of a relationship.

BEDIVERE

Bedivere was one of the original members of Arthur's warband. He was a valuable strategist and loyal friend to Arthur throughout his reign. It was Bedivere alone who comforted the king as he lay dying on the battlefield of Camlann (see the Judgement card).

In Welsh tradition, he is known as Bedwyr, the valiant "spear-wielder." Despite the loss of one hand, he was an exceptionally skilled member of the warband. It was said that he could draw blood from the wind with his spear.

Being that Bedivere was the original best friend of the king, he sometimes appears as the torn lover of Guenevere; a role that the later, literary Lancelot fulfils.

QUEEN OF SPEARS

MEANING

A woman of deep spiritual strength and understanding. She is sensitive to the well-being of others and encourages the pursuit of aspirations. A woman of dignity, charm, and knowledge. She represents independent thought, the strength of conviction, and a love of nature. Indicates generosity, learning, courage, and leadership.

REVERSED

Possessive behaviour. Invasion of privacy. Purposely withholding knowledge and assistance to heed the progress of others. The dashing of peoples' hopes and dreams with a cruel tongue. Jealousy.

DINDRANE

Dindrane was the daughter of King Pellinore and sister to Percivale. She was also the wise and virtuous guide to the Three Elect (those who achieved the Holy Grail)—Galahad, Percivale, and Bors.

Dindrane united the three after their many adventures and temptations and led them to an awaiting ship. No sooner were they aboard when wind and wave mysteriously carried them off to a second ship. Under Dindrane's instructions they boarded the second ship. There they found a marvellous sword which Dindrane explained was the "Sword of Strange Hangings." She then went on to tell them the history of the sword and the story of the Dolorous Stroke (see Ace of Spears).

Galahad was meant to wield the sword, but he found that the girdle could not hold its weight. On seeing this, Dindrane cut off her hair and used it, along with threads of gold and silk, to repair the girdle. The knights were inspired by this gesture and indebted to her knowledge and dedication to the Quest.

After returning to land, the strange adventures continued. While still in their company, Dindrane died after giving her blood to heal an ailing woman. The grieving knights placed her body upon a ship covered with black samite and set her adrift upon the sea.

KING OF SPEARS

MEANING

A mature noble man of wisdom. A voice of experience. Someone who can be relied upon for help. Strength and loyalty. A man of seasoned skills who sets high goals and continuously works to achieve them. An accomplished, generous person with a sense of humour and theatrical flair. An intuitive, just ruler. Can indicate living in a rural community.

REVERSED

A stern authority who, despite his shortcomings, sincerely does his best, as he sees fit, for those around him. One who is intolerant of attitudes and philosophies that differ from his own. A person unsympathetic to the difficulties faced by others.

KING PELLINORE

Pellinore was King of the Isles and brother to Pelles, the Fisher King. In some versions of the story he is father to Percivale, Lamorak, and Dindrane. In the romances, he has the arduous task of pursuing the Questing Beast (see Seven of Cups).

Pellinore was an influential ally of Arthur and joined him in his early battle with the rebel kings. According to some, it was Pellinore who killed King Lot during the revolt.

The sons of Lot later became Knights of the Round Table. Despite this, they continued to harbour their resentment, and bided their time awaiting an opportunity to avenge their father's death. Gawain and his brothers eventually ambushed and killed Pellinore. Predictably, his murder led to a blood feud within the Fellowship of the Round Table.

SWORDS

THE SUIT OF SWORDS

Swords (Blades, Spades) represent action, conflict, and decisive, analytical thinking.

In contrast with the intuitive intellect of the suit of Spears, Swords symbolize the discriminating thought process. Penetrating logic, decisive actions, and methods of coping with conflict are encompassed by the suit of Swords.

Some Tarot decks will differ in associating the element of fire with Swords. In my opinion, fire best fits the explosive and definite nature of the suit. Friction creates heat and leads to fire, just as it leads to the appearance of Swords in a card reading. Aside from this, the impact of fire mirrors the important constructive ability of Swords to clear dead wood from one's life.

The season of autumn, with its darkening days and hot colours, is associated with the suit of Swords.

ACE OF SWORDS

MEANING

The release of a great force. Action, conquest, and determination. Putting up an impressive fight.

The making of a firm decision which substantially impacts one's life. Prolonged suffering forges a great force which, when directed, frees one from an oppressive situation. Necessary change for the better. Deep and powerful emotions which initiate action and bring triumph.

REVERSED

Striking out at others without due cause. Entanglements, sterility, and violence. Indulging in excess and bringing about one's own destruction.

SWORD OF
STRANGE HANGINGS

The sacred sword awaits its destined master.

The magical or sacred sword is a common motif in Celtic legends. Excalibur is perhaps the most widely known sword of the Arthurian world, but it is not alone. A number of different but related swords figure in the stories, and as Galahad nears the end of his quest he is honoured with the awesome Sword of Strange Hangings.

During the Quest for the Holy Grail, Galahad, Percivale, and Bors were guided to a "Miraculous Ship" by Percivale's enlightened sister Dindrane. Within the ship they found a beautiful bed, and upon it rested a crown of gold and silk. Across its foot lay a magnificent sword, partly drawn from its scabbard. The pommel was adorned with the rarest and most brilliant of gems. The scabbard was made of a material never seen before, but which had the look of snake skin. Most curious of all were its strange hangings, which were of such poor quality as compared with the richness of the sword and scabbard, that it was doubtful that it would even hold the weight of the blade. Dindrane inspected the belt, then set about repairing it.

The sword bore an inscription warning great sorrows would befall the unworthy who presumed to draw it. Once reading these grave words, Galahad refused to touch the weapon. Dindrane announced that all were forbidden to draw it, save one. She then told her companions the story of the Dolorous Stroke and the wasting lands (see Ace of Spears). Further, she told them of Nascien, who had previously come across on the same ship. At first he had dared not draw the sword, but eventually adventure befell him and in an effort to defend himself Nascien called upon the sword. Given that he was not intended to wield the sword, the blade failed him and snapped in two. Later, King Mordrain, the wise friend of Nascien, pieced the sword together and held it intact. While in his grip, the blade miraculously knit itself back together. Mordrain then returned it to the bed where it would await the worthy Galahad.

Dindrane disclosed that the true name of the sword was the "Sword of Strange Hangings" and that the scabbard was called "Memory of Blood." With the hangings now repaired, she knelt down and girded the sword about Galahad, explaining that with this blade at his side he was truly a knight.

TWO OF SWORDS

MEANING

A moment of indecision. Blind judgement. Conforming to a traditional path without question. Uncertainty. Reaching an impasse and not knowing how one should proceed. Having to make a choice without the benefit of foresight. A clouded perception of one's options. A deadlock of equal forces. Procrastination. Stalling in hope that the best choice will become obvious.

REVERSED

Movement. Deceit. Disguised motives. A need for caution, as one is vulnerable to misleading information. Misrepresentation. A vague understanding leads to an undesirable choice.

THE KNIGHT OF TWO SWORDS

Balin strains to see what fate awaits him.

Having fled the Wasteland, Balin, the Knight of Two Swords, wandered into a strange kingdom. For three days his travels were uneventful, until he heard the deafening blow of a horn. All at once, the people of the land appeared and gathered about him. Balin was advised by their Chief Lady that if he wished to pass this way he must win a joust with a knight upon a nearby island. Despite his misgivings, Balin agreed to conform with the custom. The people of the land lent Balin a plain shield, maintaining his was too small. Next, they dressed him for battle and ferried both he and his horse across to the island. There Balin met his nameless opponent and the battle began. Their wounds were deep and both lost much blood. The weakened men both fell to the ground, where Balin then asked the knight his name. "Balan, brother of the good Knight Balin," he replied. Balin despaired at these words, realizing he had been blindly led into combat, and mortally wounded his own brother. The situation now became clear to Balan, who cried aloud, "Alas that I should ever see this day. I considered the two swords you carried, but in not recognizing the shield I thought you to be another." In his last breath, Balan explained how he had been kept against his will and made to participate in this custom that had brought their tragic deaths.

On hearing the tale of the brothers, Merlin travelled to the land and honoured their dying wish—to be buried within the same tomb (also see Seven of Swords).

THREE OF SWORDS

MEANING

Distress. Separation. An emotional outburst. Tormenting one's self with daydreams of disaster. Arguments between friends. Being haunted by the pain of the past. Fear of losing the affections of others. Anticipating the disapproval of others and allowing one's self to be held captive by the fear of their criticism, which may not transpire. A difficult period of readjustment. Undergoing the process of freeing one's self from the past.

REVERSED

Alienation. Disorientation. Mistakes made amidst confusion. Incompatibility. Pandemonium. A broken promise. The collapse of an alliance.

PALOMIDES

The Saracen Knight Palomides laments for his love Isolt.

Queen Isolt was one of the most beautiful women of the land. Many a knight and king admired her, but Tristram and Palomides truly loved her.

Tristram was the lover of the queen and friend to Palomides. While in their company Palomides kept his feelings to himself, but took every opportunity to impress Isolt. He was a brave and seasoned knight who bested many opponents on Isolt's behalf.

Palomides accompanied the lovers to the tournament of Lonazep. As they travelled, Tristram openly discussed his plan, in which he hoped to fool his friends by entering the tournament wearing a disguise. Both Tristram and Palomides fared well on the opening day, though Palomides desperately wanted to top the exploits of Tristram. On the second day, Palomides disguised himself and took the field as Tristram's opponent.

In witnessing the deception, Isolt was furious with Palomides. At the end of the day she told Tristram of the treachery of his friend. The couple then confronted Palomides, who maintained that due to Tristram's own disguise he knew not whether he was friend or foe.

Ashamed and hurt by the rebukes and rejection of Isolt, Palomides later rode off into the forest on his own. Deep within the woods he came upon a well. There he dismounted and in privacy cried for his love and lost friendship.

In the months that followed, Palomides continued to visit the sanctuary of the site. While out hunting, Tristram happened upon his old friend as he grieved by the well. This led to an open confrontation, and though Palomides cared for Tristram, he could not dismiss his love for Isolt. Given that he would no longer deny his feelings, both men were destined to go their own way. Only now there emerged a lengthy, and open, rivalry between the former friends (also see Seven of Cups).

FOUR OF SWORDS

MEANING

Recuperation. Healing. Retreating to a calm, safe environment. Respite. Leaving a stressful, chaotic situation in order to clear the mind and re-evaluate plans. Gentle soul searching. Regaining strength and direction. Being given protection and warm hospitality. Convalescing. Abandoning a hazardous lifestyle. May indicate a stay in the hospital.

REVERSED

Depression. Imprisonment or exile. Exhaustion caused by relentless turbulence. Controversy. A need for caution, as stress is apt to endanger one's health.

ISOLT OF THE WHITE HANDS

Isolt and the women of Brittany tend to Tristram's wound. Though Isolt of Ireland was married to King Mark, her heart belonged to Tristram. Despite her marriage, she and Tristram continued to meet in secrecy.

Eventually, the affair was discovered and in fear of their lives the two ran off and went into hiding. King Mark stayed hard on their heels and recaptured Isolt and brought her home, where she remained under close watch. Following the advice of others, Mark banished Tristram from Cornwall.

According to Malory's *Le Morte d'Arthur*, it was at this time, while Tristram hid in the forest, that he was wounded by a poisoned arrow. A man who claimed the knight had killed his brother happened upon Tristram in the woods, and there he took his vengeance.

The wound festered, endangering Tristram's life. Isolt was a skilled healer, though under such strict guard she was powerless to help him. Knowing that his life was further in peril by remaining in the kingdom, she secretly sent word to her lover. Isolt advised Tristram to leave Cornwall and seek out Isolt of the White Hands in Brittany who would tend his wound.

Tristram was warmly received by King Howel of Brittany and gently nursed by his daughter, Isolt of the White Hands. Here in the peaceful atmosphere, far from the reach of Mark, Tristram recuperated and was renewed in body, mind, and spirit. Relieved of the stresses that accompanied his first love, Tristram married the noble Isolt of the White Hands. Though he was grateful to her and knew her worthy of his love, Tristram could never consummate the marriage, owing to his undying love for Isolt of Ireland—Queen of Cornwall.

FIVE OF SWORDS

MEANING

Loss and regret. Having to accept one's limitations and acknowledge errors in judgement. Dishonour and destruction brought about by lack of self-control. Being shown one's weaknesses. Constructive criticism. Grieving for one's rash and belligerent actions. A reprimand. Facing and repenting unwise behaviour and its consequences. A valuable lesson, one not to be repeated.

REVERSED

A destructive, angry person, meddling in one's affairs. Malicious gossip. Sabotage. A need to watch out for the welfare of friends. Can represent a burial.

GAWAIN'S PENANCE

Gawain and his horse return to the court carrying evidence of his misdeeds.

In the Quest of the White Hart, Gawain was assigned the task of capturing the hart, while his comrades went in search of the brachet and its mistress (see Eight of Spears).

Following the bay of the hounds, Gawain's quest led him to a castle. Three of the hounds chased the hart into the hall where they set upon the animal and killed it. Gawain came upon the scene just as the enraged resident knight slew two of the hounds. Gawain's face flushed red with anger as he demanded to know why the knight had killed his dogs. "Because they have killed my hart which was given to me by my beloved," he replied. A dreadful battle began between the two knights. Gawain overcame his opponent who then cried for mercy. But the young Gawain, in his rage, unlaced the knight's helm and made ready to strike off his head. The lady of the knight entered the hall and threw herself upon her love, pleading for his life. Gawain refused to spare him and in the confusion of the struggle mistakenly slew the woman. It was a grave and shameful deed; a knight without mercy is a knight without worship.

The grieving Gawain was made to return to Arthur's court, bearing the woman's head about his neck and her body upon the mane of his horse. All were horrified at this shameful sight. Guenevere was greatly upset, and ordained that in future Gawain must fight on behalf of all ladies, no matter what their standing, and that while he lived he must remain the merciful and ever-courteous champion of all women.

SIX OF SWORDS

MEANING

Movement; journey by water. A trip abroad. Easing restrictions. The first step toward an unknown destination. Passage away from danger. A brave attempt to improve one's circumstances. Breaking free of a rut. Further effort will be needed, but progress has begun. Seeing the light at the end of the tunnel. Anticipation.

REVERSED

Solutions continue to allude one. Feeling despondent and powerless to affect the situation. The continued burden of stressful problems. Being caught in a vicious cycle of worry. Delays in travel. Having to deal with unsolicited advances and harassment.

THE EACHTRA

Arthur and his mortal raiders venture to Annwn.

The Eachtra is the Irish term used to refer to an Otherworld journey and adventure. The islands of the Otherworld (or Annwn) were generally thought to lie in the "twilight realm" to the west. Arthur and his crew travel to this enchanted land in the poem "The Spoils of Annwfn" (see the Temperance card). Under the circumstances, Arthur's Eachtra was not necessarily a pleasant one. Despite their enticing names—the Fortunate Isles or Isles of the Blest—not all of the islands were paradisal. There were many strange and wonderful variations in their natures. Some were inhabited only by women, wise and skilled healers recalling the sisterhood of Avalon. Others were isles of laughter and homes to giants, spirits, and strange creatures. There was no limit to these immortal isles nor their fantastic characters. The inhabitants were known to produce the finest wines. Owing to this, Annwn of Welsh tradition is sometimes referred to as "The Court of Intoxication."

The sublime waters of Annwn were thought to be the haunt of the mythological Barinthus, who guided mortals beyond the veil. Due to his association with Otherworldly voyages and his vast knowledge of the waters and stars, he is also called the "Navigator." Barinthus figures in the story of St. Brendan, inspiring the sixth-century Irish saint to travel the seas in search of the Land of Promise. Barinthus the Navigator sometimes appears in the Arthurian saga as the figure who guides the barge carrying the wounded king to the Isle of Avalon.

SEVEN OF SWORDS

MEANING

Inspiration. Enthusiasm. A new direction and purpose. The beginning of a new enterprise. Recent events bring the promise of brighter days to come. The instilling of hope, faith, and strength. Sensing one is on the destined path. The renewal of spirit and ambition. Following what seem to be good omens pointing the way.

REVERSED

Being given poor advice. Having to contend with armchair critics who underestimate one's dedication and skill. A lack of support. Discouraging remarks fuel one's determination.

THE SWORD IN THE STONE

Galahad draws Balin's sword from the stone.

After the death of Balin (see Two of Swords), the mastermind Merlin embedded his sword in a stone and set it to hover above the waters of a river. The stone held fast to the blade, destined to only release its grip when pulled by the knight who would achieve the Holy Grail. Over the years, the stone drifted downstream to arrive at Arthur's court, where Merlin's vision would come to pass.

On the feast of Pentecost, a great marvel befell the court. A squire reported to Arthur that a stone of red marble had appeared in the river below, and embedded in the stone was an ornate sword. Arthur gathered the Fellowship and went to see for himself.

Lancelot beheld the sword, then called his king aside. He then went on to explain to Arthur that when the rightful knight succeeded in pulling the sword from the stone, it would herald the beginning of the Quest for the Holy Grail. Knowing he was not the destined knight, Lancelot refused to try to draw the sword. On Arthur's bidding, both Gawain and Percivale tried their hand and failed. Having seen the "marvel" Kay urged all to return to the hall to dine.

As they sat down, the shutters and doors of the Castle mysteriously shut by their own accord. There then appeared a man of great age, and at his side a handsome young knight. The knight carried no sword or shield, only a scabbard. The old man introduced the young knight as Galahad the Desired Knight. Thereupon he led Galahad to his destined seat at the Round Table. Having done his duty, the old man then left the court. Suspecting that the Quest awaited this knight, Arthur led the newcomer to the river's edge. On seeing the sword, Galahad knew the task to be his. The young knight looked to the heavens, then drew the sword as if nothing held it. He sheathed the blade within his scabbard; the dawn of the Quest had come.

EIGHT OF SWORDS

MEANING

Feeling bound and trapped. Being held at a disadvantage. Inability to free one's self from a difficult situation. Having to rely on the judgement of others. Slander. Domination. Calamity and regret. Personal effort and courage are needed to take advantage of a temporary route of escape. Approaching the end of adversity.

REVERSED

Senseless tragedy. Frustration. Ceaseless pressures. Depression. Treachery and betrayal. Unintentionally hurting loved ones. Continuing conflict.

GUENEVERE AT THE STAKE

Golden chains bind the High Queen to her doom.

For the many years that Lancelot and Guenevere were lovers, Arthur had done his best to overlook the affair. Despite the hurt and humiliation, he continued to love his queen and his best friend. Though rumours had circulated there was no proof of adultery, but Mordred set about to change this. By bringing the affair out in the open for all to see, Mordred put the king in a desperate position. The new religion did not allow the Queen to take lovers, and to do so was considered an offense to the king. Being that Guenevere was the wife of the High King, her betrayal was considered an act of high treason—punishable by death.

Though Arthur did all he could to stall the sentence, Mordred led the people in howls of disgust, demanding that Arthur fulfil his obligation as king. Guenevere was damned to burn at the stake.

As the fateful moment arrived and the queen was bound to the stake, Lancelot and his band rushed upon the scene and frantically hacked their way to the queen. Lancelot succeeded in rescuing his beloved and carried her to safety. Guenevere's life had been saved, but with tragic results. In his frenzy, Lancelot had killed many of his friends, including the much-loved Gareth. The formidable Gawain sought his former friend to avenge the death of his brothers. With this tragedy, blood feuds erupted and split the Fellowship of the Round Table.

NINE OF SWORDS

NINE OF SWORDS

LILY MAID
OF ASTOLAT

MEANING

Heartache. Disappointment. Pining for a loved one. Misery. Longing.
Fretful dreams and obsessions taking their toll on one's health. Suffering
that arises in the mind rather than environment. Depression blinding
one to the possibilities and beauty that surrounds one. Mental anguish
and tears. Believing one cannot go on. Making matters worse by suffering
in silence.

REVERSED

Warranted suspicion and doubt. Cruel gossip. Undergoing a painful phase
of retrospection before moving on with life. Learning to focus on positive
thoughts which lift one out of the pit of despair.

LILY MAID OF ASTOLAT

The gentle waters carry the frail Elaine to her beloved.

Elaine of Astolat met Lancelot when he lodged in her father's house. It was not long before Elaine became infatuated with the famous knight. While staying under her father's roof, Lancelot began planning a disguise with which he hoped to fool his fellow knights in an upcoming tournament. It was the custom for the knights of the day to display a token of their lady when they entered the tournament. Thinking it would add to the disguise, Lancelot agreed to wear the scarlet sleeve belonging to Elaine. This gesture only served to fuel her passion. However, Lancelot was soon glad for her kindness, as after being seriously injured it was Elaine who patiently nursed him back to health. All this time the maid's love deepened, while Lancelot remained unaware of her feelings.

When the day came for Lancelot to return to the court, Elaine disclosed her undying love. Lancelot did his utmost to console the maid, but he could not reciprocate her love, as his heart belonged to Guenevere alone.

With his departure Elaine's heart broke. She refused to eat, and over the days began to waste away; the Lily Maid only wished to die.

Elaine's despairing father was called to her bedside where she instructed him to make ready a barge and choose a trusted man to guide it. She then asked that she be placed within the barge and set to drift downstream. All was done as Elaine had instructed.

The river carried the Lily Maid to Arthur's court as she had intended. A crowd gathered to look upon the beautiful young woman whose skin was as white as a lily.

Word of the maid reached Lancelot, who, on beholding the cold body, remembered the fair Elaine. In her hand lay a scroll telling of her love, which had been the cause of her death. The king read her story and dying wish aloud. All eyes turned to Lancelot, whose heart was heavy with sorrow. He honoured the Lily Maid's dying wish in offering the mass penny and burying her frail body.

The story may seem familiar to some owing to Tennyson's poem "The Lady of Shalott." Tennyson drew from an Italian source, and we conclude from the poet's own remarks that at that time he was unaware of the story of the Maid of Astolat.

TEN OF SWORDS

MEANING

Troubles. Conflict. The underlying animosity of the past gives way to an all-out offensive. The climax and end of a chapter. This card generally indicates strife and division within a community.

    Unfortunate events spark intense conflict. A showdown. The clash of ideas. Release and the destruction of the old order. The inevitable exhaustion of a cycle gives way to a new era.

REVERSED

Overcoming a revolt. Retaining one's position, if only temporarily. Having a decisive advantage over an opponent. Evading disaster.

CAMLANN

The dark day cometh when brother turns against brother.

Following the bloodshed of Guenevere's rescue (see Eight of Swords), Lancelot and his companions released the queen to Arthur and made their way to France. There Lancelot began to claim some of Arthur's lands for himself. In order to arraign the rebellious Lancelot, Arthur had to leave Britain and journey to Gaul.

The king appointed Mordred to rule in his absence. By all rights Mordred was entitled to the position, but Arthur would have cause to regret his choice.

Mordred was of ambitious character, and once the king was safely overseas he began to spread false news of Arthur's death. Not knowing what was to come, Guenevere barricaded herself in the Tower of London, while Mordred fuelled the unrest.

Word reached Arthur, who immediately returned to Britain. By this time, Mordred had taken advantage of the recent controversy surrounding the Fellowship and had succeeded in winning some support. He had also managed to strike a deal with the Saxons, who now rallied to his cause.

The arrival of Arthur dispelled reports of his death, but his mere presence was not enough to subdue the revolt. Some versions say that the two sides agreed to meet and discuss a compromise, but by an unfortunate mishap (see Page of Swords) the battle broke out.

The tragic battle of Camlann was to be the last of Arthur and his Fellowship. His battle-weary force fought bravely against a much larger host. There was to be no victor in this conflict, as both leaders perished. Mordred inflicted Arthur's fatal wound and then died at the king's hand.

Few survived this dark day that brought the end to a glorious reign.

PAGE OF SWORDS

MEANING

Insight. Receiving first-hand knowledge of a consequential matter. Overseeing confidential affairs. A young, active person with a sharp mind and gift for learning secrets. A clever spy. An inconspicuous witness to important events. Clandestine activities. An unexpected plot twist. A vigilant supporter who learns much on behalf of friends.

REVERSED

An elusive opponent. A stealthy troublemaker. A person who is capable of luring one into a false sense of security. A turncoat.

THE ADDER

The serpent is an ancient totem of wisdom, embodying profound archaic knowledge of the underworld. Hidden activities, particularly of the subconscious, are often symbolized by the serpent and its unyielding stare.

The serpent/dragon plays timekeeper in the Arthurian cycle. The comet, shaped as a winged serpent, heralds the dawn of the Pendragon reign (see the Star card), while the adder brings it to a close.

Arthur had agreed to meet with Mordred to discuss a treaty. Both leaders suspected a trap and warned their men to watch for signs of treachery. At the perilous moment when Arthur and Mordred stood face to face, a nearby soldier was startled by an adder. He drew his sword to kill the snake; the flash of the blade alarmed both sides who then fell into battle.

KNIGHT OF SWORDS

MEANING

A determined, intelligent young man. One who bravely faces opposition. A valiant champion of human rights. A skilled man with strong convictions. One who may be overeager to display heroics which cause him to misjudge the situation. A forthright person who refuses to compromise his principles.

REVERSED

An aggressive, rash young man who enjoys conflict. One with a high opinion of himself. A man with little respect for others, particularly women. A smug, chauvinistic fool.

GAWAIN

Gawain of Orkney was the eldest son of King Lot and Morgause (sometimes Anna), the half-sister of Arthur.

In Welsh tradition, he bears the name Gwalchmei—"Hawk (or falcon) of May," and is the son of Anna and Llew ap Kynfarch.

The early portraits of Gawain depict a valiant knight endowed with a supernatural strength that increases with the height of the sun. Aside from his solar power, his pre-Christian origins are also reflected in his charge as "Knight of the Goddess." Knowing this, it is not surprising that the Faery are drawn to Gawain. It would seem that he is their favoured knight whom they artfully test throughout his adventures (see Ten of Spears and Nine of Shields).

Gawain's original courteous manner is sometimes disregarded and he is portrayed as a disrupter rather than leader who is overly fond of women and wine. Despite this fall from grace, Gawain generally maintains his close relationship with his uncle, the High King.

QUEEN OF SWORDS

MEANING

A very clever woman with an uncanny perception. She is discreet, yet ambitious, and more than capable of winning success. Intelligent and versatile, she often outwits those who oppose her. A woman who firmly believes knowledge is power. Despite her capabilities, she can represent a woman embittered by the past. The Queen of Swords can indicate separation, widowhood, or financial instability.

REVERSED

A vengeful woman who plots, but lacks the skill to bring about her devious ends. An intolerant, malicious woman driven by jealousy. A steadfast enemy.

MORGAUSE

Morgause was the daughter of Igraine and her first husband, Gorlois, the Duke of Cornwall. By her birth, Morgause was full sister to Morgan and half-sister to Arthur.

Much like Morgan, Morgause was a law unto herself. Her independent ways and habit of taking lovers led her to be given the same unseemly reputation as her liberated sister. Morgause wed the rebel, King Lot of Orkney. She bore five sons—Gawain, Gaheris, Agravain, Gareth, and Mordred—all of whom joined Arthur at his court. Though it is absent in earlier versions, the story developed to include an incestuous relationship between Morgause and Arthur, who was said to be unaware of their blood ties at the time. Their alleged union begat Mordred, and so ultimately this sin became the convenient reason for the fall of Arthur.

After her husband's death, Morgause spent much of her time ruling her lands and raising her sons. It was said that Arthur dreaded her visits as they sowed discord amongst the knights, who competed for the beauty's attention. While on one of her occasional visits to the court, Morgause took Lamorak, the young son of Pellinore, to be her lover. Pellinore, by some accounts, was the man who had killed King Lot in Arthur's early battle with the rebel kings.

In light of this, Lot's sons saw their mother's behaviour as a disgrace to their father's memory. Thinking that his mother had betrayed her clan, Gaheris slew both lovers as they lay in her bed.

KING OF SWORDS

MEANING

A somewhat unpredictable leader who strives to implement revolutionary ideas. A man with power enough to enforce change. An authority figure who has secured his standing, but continues to seek promotion. One who may be ruthless and daring in attaining his ambitions. A man with a commanding presence. An experienced person who possesses a sharp, analytical mind.

REVERSED

One who is intent on destruction. A person of power who employs cruel methods to retain supremacy. An unfavourable outcome of a legal matter. Heavy-handed authority.

MORDRED

Mordred, or Medraut, was the son of Morgause (sometimes Anna or Morgan) and nephew to Arthur. The French romances make him out to be the incestuous offspring of Arthur and Morgause; though this horror is absent in many accounts, it continues to impact and colour the reputation of Mordred.

Once Mordred came of age, his mother sent him to join his brothers at Arthur's court. Initially, Mordred was considered to be a loyal supporter of the king, but after witnessing the reality of his court, Mordred became disillusioned. In an effort to rid the court of its seamy side, Mordred began to expose its long-guarded secrets. He began with the queen's affair with Lancelot, the ramifications of which would cause the Fellowship to self-destruct and Mordred to reach for the throne (see Ten of Swords).

At his worst, Mordred is portrayed as the traitorous villain who leads a revolt against and dies with Arthur. At best, he has a legitimate claim to the throne as son of the king's sister, and seeks to replace the fading Arthur and lead the people into a new era.

The character of Mordred may be based on the historical figure Medraut, who is recorded as having died in the battle of Camlann in A.D. 539. Whether he opposed or fought alongside Arthur in this battle is not known.

CUPS

THE SUIT OF CUPS

Cups (Cauldrons, Vessels, etc.) represent the lifeforce or creative energy. Cups are symbolic of the womb and are the feminine counterpart to the masculine Spear. The suit indicates emotional states and responses, creation, fertility, love, and fantasy.

The happiness, fulfilment, and contentment that the suit of Cups represents depend greatly on one's inner emotional well-being and how one perceives the world. The well-known question "Is the cup half full or half empty?" illustrates this concept.

The image of the cup or cauldron is symbolic of the divine essence which is the foundation of our being and the source of our creativity, imagination, compassion, and love.

The suit of Cups is associated with water—the source of life— and the season of summer.

ACE OF CUPS

MEANING

Abundance. Happiness, nourishment, and protection. The beginning of a fulfilling, worthwhile project or cycle in life. Contentment, joy, and satisfaction. Lending one's skills to further a noble cause. Goodwill and divine inspiration. Fertility and productivity. Following a higher call. Receptivity to a higher plane. Receiving the fruits of past kindness.

REVERSED

Emotional bruises. Loss of hope. Fatigue and loneliness. Disappointment in love. Emotional instability. Barrenness. Longing for but unable to envision what would bring one happiness. Being stuck in an emotional rut.

THE HOLY GRAIL

Blessed are those who witness the marvel of the Holy Grail.

If one were to think of the Holy Grail as merely the material object of the Quest, all hope of enlightenment is lost. To benefit from and understand the enduring fascination of the legend, the Grail must take on its higher significance. Though we may not comprehend its mysteries, if the Grail is thought of as the sacrosanct symbol of the Divine presence, the Quest may begin. In essence, the Grail is ever-present, though not all recognize it.

All nature can be considered a manifestation of the Grail and its omnipotent water. Judging by our internal response, one may suspect that music and art are gifts of the Grail—and a glimpse of the grace and beauty which lies beyond.

Though the knights covered physical distance in their search, their true Quest was of an inner nature. Their adventures served as catalysts, tempering, stressing, and accelerating their development until eventually they transgressed their limitations of thought, allowing the light to flood in. In this expansion and temporary dissolution of the self, one becomes immersed in the spirit of the Grail, absorbing (but not necessarily understanding) its mysteries. This is the ultimate mystical experience and communion sought by the knights and many souls of past and present.

The Grail has a number of symbolic guises, some of which are the chalice, cauldron, dish, or platter. Celtic legends abound of Otherworld cauldrons whose attributes closely resemble those of the Grail. The cauldrons of the Celtic tales were the source of inspiration and unearthly knowledge. Some were said to have the power to restore life and provide enough food to sustain entire communities. The Cauldron of Plenty motif survives in the Christianized version of the Arthurian legend, with the Grail appearing as a food-providing vessel that feeds the entire Fellowship of the Round Table. The similarities have led some to believe that our conception of the Grail is a blend of the Pagan Celtic cauldron and the Christian chalice of the Last Supper and that which caught the blood of Christ.

The Grail image of the Ace of Cups is my personal impression and differs somewhat from the gold, gem-studded chalice traditionally depicted. At first glance one will recognize the chalice, while the vessel itself is the dark blue Cauldron of Annwn (see the Temperance card). The cauldron is cradled within the branches of the Tree of Life, whose trunk forms the stem, reaching up from its earthly roots to symbolically connect heaven and earth. A six-winged seraph hovers above the Grail, while the nine priestesses of Celtic tradition attend below.

TWO OF CUPS

MEANING

Love. Union. Rapport. The forming of strong emotional bonds. Mutual understanding and sympathy. The sharing of a common experience. Joy and contentment. Confiding in another. Emotional stability within a romantic relationship. A harmonious domestic life. The beginning of a trusted partnership. Pleasure and comfort. Can indicate falling in love, engagement, or marriage.

REVERSED

An empty relationship. An incompatible combination. Quarrels and emotional pain. False promises. Betrayal of confidence. Separation, divorce, and emotionally charged conflicts.

TRISTRAM & ISOLT

The potion seals the fated love of Tristram and Isolt.

As a young man, Tristram of Lyonesse left his homeland in search of adventure. His travels brought him to Cornwall, ruled by his uncle, King Mark. Mark had been at war with Ireland, and during Tristram's stay, Morholt of Ireland arrived in Cornwall, demanding a tribute from the king. Tristram fought Morholt in single combat and killed the more experienced warrior. However, Morholt's weapons had been tipped with poison and Tristram weakened. Thinking his end to be near, Tristram asked to be set adrift upon the sea. The boat carried him to Ireland where Isolt and her women found and nursed the stranger. During his recovery, Tristram taught Isolt how to play the harp, and over time they became fond of one another.

Isolt's father announced that whoever could rid the land of a terrible dragon would receive the hand of his daughter in marriage. Tristram thought to win Isolt on behalf of King Mark, who had been seeking a wife. Tristram took up the challenge and succeeded in killing the dragon. It was at this time that Isolt saw Tristram's sword, and recognized the chipped blade she knew to have killed Morholt, her uncle. Isolt's heart turned from Tristram, but despite her rage she kept her secret, knowing that if she were to speak of this she would be given in marriage to a man she detested.

Tristram escorted the beautiful Irish princess to Cornwall. Upon this journey the couple were accidentally given a love potion, which had been intended for King Mark and Isolt. The love it induced overwhelmed the resentment Isolt held for her escort, who then became her lover.

After her marriage, Isolt continued her affair with Tristram. Eventually, they were exposed and after many scandals Tristram went into exile in Brittany, where he married Isolt of the White Hands (see Four of Swords). When in Brittany, Tristram again received a poisonous wound. Isolt of the White Hands was unable to slow the infection, so Tristram asked for the help of Isolt of Ireland who had cured him years before. A ship was sent to Cornwall to bring Isolt. Tristram instructed the crew to hoist white sails if Isolt returned with them, and black if she did not. In the time it took the ship to return, Tristram's condition deteriorated. The knight was near death as the ship entered the harbour. Tristram looked to his wife, who watched from the window, and asked her what colour were the sails. Knowing her husband to still love Isolt, the hurt Isolt of Brittany answered—black. At this response Tristram died in despair. Isolt came ashore and hurried to the bedside of her love. On finding herself too late, Isolt ran herself upon Tristram's sword. Both bodies were returned to Cornwall, where they were laid to rest alongside each other. Two trees later grew upon and intertwined above the lover's graves.

THREE OF CUPS

MEANING

A celebration of good fortune. Acknowledging blessings. A joyous social occasion. Festivities, bounty, fulfilment, and happiness. The exchanging of gifts. The realization of a dream. Good health and harmony. Friendship and solidarity. Enjoying the company of others. Creativity, fertility, and good cheer.

REVERSED

A waste of resources. Carelessness. Overindulgence. Irresponsible, short-sighted behaviour. The end of a prosperous cycle. Greed. Exploiting the good will of others. An unappreciative recipient.

THE DRESSING OF THE SACRED SPRING

Homage is paid to the benevolent spirit of the spring.

Nature worship was at the heart of the Celtic Pagan religion. The Celts believed the Divine to be inherent in the landscape, with every feature inhabited by the spirits of nature. To the early Celts, springs, rivers, and lakes of the Isle of the Mighty were the dwelling places of the spirits of water. For this reason many streams (especially springs) were considered sacred sites, each with its individual guardian spirit.

The fresh waters that sprung from the earth were thought to carry gifts from the underworld—cures for the sick, and in some instances, knowledge, inspiration, and future sight. Some wells were said to restore life; if offended, the spirit would also take life, rising up and drowning the culprit.

Given that the spirits of water were generally considered feminine, the dressing, rites, and offerings to the goddess of the spring are thought to have been performed by women. This tradition, though somewhat modified, continues to be practiced in May or Midsummer in some parts of Britain. The wells were dressed with flowers, beads, shells, and other decorative natural treasures.

Judging by the numerous bent pins found in wells, pins were a popular offering. The swords, shields, and other rich objects found in the beds of rivers, lakes, and wells are a testament to the importance of the aqua goddesses.

The veneration of the well continues in the Arthurian world, where the fountain often appears with the "Ageless Elders" (the Fay of Eternal Youth) and remains the favoured site of the broken-hearted. Though the springs later took on a Christian semblance, some of the early Celtic practices continued. In the modern world, clooties (small swatches of cloth) are still tied to neighbouring trees or left to rot near the spring, and the common custom of dropping a coin into a well echoes the early votive offerings of the pre-Christian Celts.

FOUR OF CUPS

MEANING

Boredom. Tedium. An uninspired lifestyle. Growing weary of the day-to-day routine. No longer finding pleasure in activities one used to enjoy. Lack of motivation. Apathy. Having achieved a goal, but finding limited comforts in its fruits. Disgust and disillusionment.

A vision that has materialized, reached its pinnacle, and now decays. The inability to recognize an opportunity or higher goal.

REVERSED

Returning ambition. Renewed vigor. The taking of a new direction. Successful adjustment to a new lifestyle. Meeting new people and being introduced to new ideas.

THE FADING FELLOWSHIP

Arthur's once disciplined warband shows signs of decay.

Having won a victory at Mount Badon, Arthur faced the challenge of completing the work of restoration that Ambrosius had begun.

Over the years, Arthur worked tirelessly to rebuild Britain to the glory she had once known. Buildings were repaired and new laws passed to protect and bring order to the land. Arthur travelled to the more remote, neglected realms, securing alliances and local administrative systems to keep the peace in his absence. This post-Badonic period allowed the society and the economy to recover and the Christian church to flourish.

According to legend, Arthur makes a transition from warrior to king. His efforts are no longer on the battlefield, but rather the political arena. Despite the realization of peace in his land, the monotony of his domestic duties hang heavy on the king. The lustre of the Fellowship of the Round Table begins to tarnish. With no immediate threat to unite them, quarrels break out amongst the knights. Endless days of revelry disgust some of the men, who then leave the court to tend to their own lands. Though nobles throughout the kingdom continue to send their sons to Arthur's care, they soon become disillusioned by what they find. The king looked to busy his men with campaigns abroad, but this neither fulfilled him nor satisfied his men.

The weary cycle eventually came to an end when the apparition of the Grail appeared above the Round Table upon a shaft of light. In witnessing this marvel, all the knights pledged to seek to learn its mysteries for a year and a day, and longer if need be. This mysterious event renewed the solidarity and dedication of the Fellowship of the Round Table as they went in search of the Grail.

FIVE OF CUPS

MEANING

Partial loss. Loneliness, disappointment, and sorrow. Heartache. Rejection. An empty marriage or romance. Being let down. Unfulfilled hopes and dreams. An unexpected change of plans. Unfair treatment from others. Frustration. A need to acknowledge a loss and focus on what blessings one still has.

REVERSED

Reunion with an old friend or lover. Hope of a new relationship. An unexpected gift or inheritance. A need to balance emotions so one does not project what one would like to see rather than what is really there.

LANCELOT & ELAINE

Elaine looks on as Lancelot longs for his old love.

Elaine of Corbenic was the daughter of King Pelles—the Keeper of the Grail. She loved Lancelot all of her days and gave birth to his son, Galahad. Lancelot acknowledged the child, but claimed he had been tricked into sleeping with Elaine by the craft of her lady-in-waiting, the enchantress Brisen. When Guenevere found the couple in bed together, she banished both from the court, which drove the grief-stricken Lancelot mad (see the Hermit card).

When Lancelot's sanity returned, he found himself in the keeping of Elaine and her kin. For two weeks, Elaine took care of her love while he regained his strength. Ashamed of how he had treated her in the past, Lancelot asked Elaine for her forgiveness, which was freely given. In a further effort to make amends, Lancelot asked after their child. Elaine was encouraged by Lancelot's interest, and when he asked if she thought her father would give them a castle, Elaine happily approached the king. Wishing his daughter to be happy, Pelles was generous to the couple, giving them the Castle of Bliant and twenty noble ladies and ten knights.

Lancelot was most pleased with his new home, and renamed it Joyous Isle. Elaine went to great pains to make Lancelot happy, and yet every day he would look in the direction of Arthur's court. Elaine watched helplessly as Lancelot pined for Guenevere.

Eventually the fateful day that Elaine had long dreaded arrived. Lancelot met up with Percivale and Ector, and joined them on their journey to Arthur's court, leaving Elaine with their son, and sorrow.

SIX OF CUPS

MEANING

Nostalgia. A time of reflection and reliving fond memories of bygone days. Drawing nourishment and comfort from recalling playful days of childhood. Old friends re-enter one's life, bringing pleasant surprises. Efforts of the past come to fruition. Happiness as a result of previous kindness. Meeting aspects of the past.

REVERSED

An unhealthy attachment to the past prevents one from appreciating the present. Having to contend with frightening and debilitating memories of childhood. Insecurity and longing for protection.

IN ECTOR'S KEEPING

In times past there were days of play.

After the marriage of Uther and Igraine, Morgause (or Anna) left her mother's side and became the wife of King Lot. Morgan was placed in the care of the sisterhood of Avalon, and Arthur was hidden away by Merlin. The sage wisely kept the boy's identity a secret, fearing those who would wish harm on Uther's son. It was said that Merlin travelled to the home of Sir Ector and his family. This remote land and its loyal family made for a secure foster home for Arthur.

Fosterage was a common practice of the noble blood. Children would often stay with the foster family until they came of age, which was generally fourteen for girls and seventeen for boys.

In the case of Arthur, no formal arrangements had been made, and some say that Ector and his wife knew not of Arthur's royal blood. But on the bidding of Merlin, the family accepted the boy.

While in Ector's keeping, Arthur enjoyed a freedom he would never know again. Most thought him just one of the many royal bastards (as did Arthur himself), which meant his movements were no more restricted than those of his foster brother Kay. Being no more privileged than his companions, Arthur's childhood instilled him with a sense of fair play and honour. Kay and Arthur were given an education and made to study literature, foreign languages, poetry, music, and the arts of war, after which they were free to roam and enjoy childhood pastimes.

Arthur was a likeable boy who later cherished his years and friendships made while in the care of Sir Ector.

SEVEN OF CUPS

MEANING

A highly active imagination. Humour. Amusing daydreams. Strong and sometimes conflicting desires. A need to temper fantasy with practicality and sincere effort, if hopes and wishes are to become more than pipe dreams. Witnessing or being caught up in bizarre events. Feeling disoriented. Can reflect the effect of drugs and alcohol.

REVERSED

Accurate perception. Height of creativity. The making of a positive, realistic commitment. Organization. A clear understanding of true desires. Harnessing all of one's energy and channelling it into a worthwhile, imaginative cause.

THE QUESTING BEAST

The Questing Beast bays upon the morning air, encouraging the wild imaginings of its seekers.

The Questing Beast (or Beast Glatisant) is a fantastic and bizarre creature who haunted the forests of Britain. It was said to have the head of a serpent, the body of a leopard, and cloven hooves. From its belly came a deafening noise likened to that of thirty hounds. Some claimed the beast was the offspring of a mortal woman who had been torn apart by a pack of hounds.

Arthur encountered the extraordinary creature in the early days of his reign. Having broken from a hunt, the king laid down beside a spring and drifted to sleep. Arthur woke at the sound of what he thought were approaching hounds. The king looked on as the strangest of beasts emerged from the woods and began to drink from the well. Only when the beast drank did the dreadful bays cease. With its thirst quenched the creature fled, and once again the forest was filled with the sound of its bays.

The bewildered Arthur then turned to see Pellinore stumble out of the woods, whence the beast had come. Pellinore hurriedly explained that he was in pursuit of the beast, and asked if he might have Arthur's horse. The king handed Pellinore the reigns and wished him well on his quest. At this, Pellinore turned to the king and told him how he had relentlessly pursued the beast for the past year, and would do so until he achieved it, or met his death. Despite his dedication, Pellinore never did win the beast. After Pellinore's death, Palomides took up the peculiar quest and endlessly followed the fantastic creature.

EIGHT OF CUPS

MEANING

Abandoning a path. A change of plans. Learning that things are not always as they seem. Escaping an unhealthy situation. Taking the initiative to redirect one's life. Heeding warnings. Recognizing that one has made a wrong turn in the search for fulfilment. Moving on. Refusing to accept defeat. Reworking priorities and enacting a congruent lifestyle.

REVERSED

Being drawn into a morass of problems. Trying to convince one's self that one ought to be happy with what has already been attained. Willingly suffering a detrimental situation. Denying that a negative relationship exists. Living under threats.

CHAPEL PERILOUS

The black hand of Chapel Perilous extinguishes the light.

The sinister tale of Chapel Perilous was said to embody one of the mysteries of the Grail—a secret which no one may speak of without inviting great peril.

The name and sex of the hero/heroine, as well as the experiences and details of the foreboding Chapel, differ somewhat with each version of the Grail romances. In the story of Gawain, the questing knight rode alone in search of the Grail Castle. As he passed through a forest, a storm began to brew overhead. Gawain rode on, but the terrific storm overtook him. The sky blackened; the trees moaned under the fierce wind. The horseman's spirits rose when he saw a light in the distance. He followed the beacon to a crossroads deep in the heart of the forest. There before him stood a chapel, from where the light shone through an open door. Thinking he had found shelter for the night, Gawain entered the Perilous Chapel. No cloth covered the altar; it was bare, save for a giant golden candle. Gawain studied the room, then lifted his eyes to the window above the altar. To his horror, a giant, hideous black hand reached through the window. At this moment a deafening voice rose, threatening and lamenting until it shook the structure and the ground beneath him. Gawain's horse trembled then shied as the black hand reached further and extinguished the light. The knight fought to keep his senses, crossed himself, and fled. Once they were clear of the chapel the storm subsided and gave way to calm skies, allowing horse and rider to travel deep into the night.

NINE OF CUPS

MEANING

Success. Accomplishment. Good health. Kindness and compassion. Overcoming obstacles. Restored peace and happiness. Gratitude and good will. Relief and joyous celebrations. A team, united in vision, makes success a reality. Sharing blessings with others. Emotional well-being. The dawn of dreams. Great satisfaction in a task well done.

REVERSED

Limited rewards for one's efforts. Events not quite living up to one's expectations. Minor errors spoil the fruit of one's labour.

THE HEALING OF THE MAIMED KING

The Wasteland is renewed with the healing of its king.

Nearing the end of their Quest, Galahad, Percivale, and Bors landed on the shores of the Wasteland. There they mounted the horses that awaited them and sought out King Pelles. The people of the wasting land rejoiced at the sight of the three knights, believing their suffering to be near its end. Pelles was overjoyed to see his grandson, but was too weakened by his wound to rise from his bier.

Knowing what would follow their arrival, the wounded king asked to be left alone with Galahad and his companions. All became deathly still, then a warm, scented breeze washed over the knights—it was the breath of heaven. A brilliant light burst forth, filling the air with strains of unearthly music. The king's eyes softened. The three knights looked on in awe as a procession of graceful figures came forth from the light. First came two figures bearing two candles; the third bore a cloth of red samite; the fourth bore the sacred lance, and a dish to catch the blood that fell from its tip. Lastly came the Grail, veiled from the mortal eyes that would not bear its splendour. The company knew themselves to be in the presence of the Divine. All three knights were overcome with a sense of beauty and bliss.

A disembodied voice instructed Galahad to approach and drink from the Grail. As the knight lifted the veil and looked into the mystery, all his desire for earthly life drained from him. At the bidding of the voice, Galahad turned from the Grail, touched his fingers to the blood of the spear, and then placed his hand over the wound of the king. At once, the flesh healed of itself. Thereupon, the Wasteland burst forth in bloom. The Maimed King was whole, and free from all pain. Once again birds sang, and green leaves chattered in the winds.

TEN OF CUPS

MEANING

Home and happiness. Completion, contentment, and blessings. A comfortable and secure domestic life. A peaceful, warm existence. Achieving emotional fulfilment. Lasting success. The successful completion of a long-term goal. Mounting self-esteem. Gaining the respect of one's community. Virtue and honour.

REVERSED

Strife within the home. Living within a restrictive, negative atmosphere. Pettiness and family feuds. Loss of patience. Antisocial behaviour. Disappointment and loss of social standing.

CORBENIC

Enchantment doth reveal the Castle of the Grail.

Due to the Otherworldly nature of the Grail Castle, it has no permanent location. No matter what direction one travels, it will appear to those worthy and destined to witness its marvels. The early versions of the legend refer to the castle as the Castle of the Maimed King—the castle that the young and innocent Percivale encounters, the onset of his career. The castle later takes on the name Corbenic, and with it, its grandeur increases from that of a keep, or modest sanctuary of the Grail guardians, to a magnificent castle with many inhabitants. Storytellers of the past have envisioned the castle to lie within a wide range of landscapes, from gentle valleys to rugged coastlines. The one feature that remains consistent is the presence of water, whether it be strong seas, calm lakes, or a series of moats.

Though Lancelot did not achieve the Quest, he was permitted to enter Corbenic on two occasions. The first of which was when he had lost his sanity, was found by Elaine, and healed by the power of the Grail. Lancelot's second visit was during the time of the Quest, when all of Arthur's knights sought the Castle of the Grail. Lancelot had been considered the best, or "Flower of Knights," and yet his sinful affair with the queen prevented him from achieving the Grail, leaving the role of hero to be fulfilled by his virtuous son. Lancelot did, however, come to understand that the search for the Grail Castle was a spiritual journey. This revelation led the knight to give up his futile wandering and turn to the lifestyle of a hermit.

One night, a mysterious, unmanned ship appeared out of the darkness. Lancelot boarded the vessel, which carried him to the towering Castle of Corbenic. As the anxious knight stood before the castle, a voice broke the silence and bade him enter. Once he was within its walls, the air filled with divine music. The door before him opened, releasing the brilliant light and revealing the high mass. The voice forbid Lancelot to enter the chamber on account of his sin, but the knight could not help but step forward. At once he was struck down by a bolt of lightning, and left stranded between life and death. Four-and-twenty days passed before Lancelot regained consciousness. On waking he remembered the vision with which he had been blessed. Knowing now that he would not be the one to achieve the Quest, Lancelot left Corbenic, never to return.

THE PAGE OF CUPS

MEANING

An imaginative, reflective person who offers valuable insights. A young, studious visionary whose talents are beginning to bloom. A comforting, inspiring friend who is generous with his or her ideas. A sensitive and loyal employee. The arrival of heart-warming news. The beginning of a creative project or birth of a child.

REVERSED

False flattery and seduction. One who claims to be an artist, but lacks depth and discipline. A person capable of deceiving one into believing he or she is something they are not.

THE SALMON

The salmon was believed by the Celts to be the oldest and wisest of all living things, having gained its great wisdom from the Nuts of Knowledge. The nine hazelnuts of wisdom were dropped into the waters of Segais Well. There the nuts created bubbles of inspiration, attracting the salmon known as Fintan, who then ate the Nuts of Knowledge. Fintan was later caught by the druid Finegas, who gave the fish to Fionn Mac-Cumhail to prepare. Much like Gwion of the story of Taliesin, Fionn burnt his fingers while cooking the fish. On licking his fingers he became endowed with the Great Wisdom.

The fish has long been a symbol of spiritual life, representing the high mystic knowledge which can only be attained and appreciated by the intuitive, emotional self.

THE KNIGHT OF CUPS

MEANING

An approaching opportunity for advancement. A tempting proposal which deserves serious consideration. An enthusiastic, active person who introduces one to new philosophies. A well-mannered, romantic man of high morals. One who constantly challenges himself. A person who genuinely appreciates the arts. A romantic interlude or marriage proposal. An unexpected gift.

REVERSED

Meeting a rival in a romantic situation. An exposed affair brings troublesome repercussions. Being the target of false malicious gossip. Trickery. Falling prey to another's wiles.

GALAHAD

Galahad was the son of Lancelot and Elaine of Corbenic. In being the grandson of the Grail Guardian and the son of the world's best knight, Galahad was the perfect knight—the messianic literary figure, created to be the stainless hero of the Grail Quest.

At a young age Galahad was placed in care of the Grail King's sister, and raised in a nunnery. Once he reached the age of fifteen, the sisters summoned Lancelot, asking that he knight the unknown boy. Lancelot agreed, knighted Galahad, then returned to the court, without suspecting that the young man was his son.

The following day Galahad was escorted to Arthur's court by an old man, who introduced him to the king and his Fellowship.

There remained one vacant seat at the Round Table, which was known as the Perilous Seat. None could rest in this seat, save the knight destined to achieve the Holy Grail. Percivale's previous attempt to sit in it brought darkness upon the court and caused stone to split. A disembodied voice then condemned the act, and Arthur, for allowing it.

The wise old man lifted the cloth that covered the Perilous Seat to reveal newly painted letters that read "This is the siege of Galahad." On the old man's bidding, Galahad sat securely in the Perilous Seat.

After witnessing this marvel, the Knights of the Round Table made the newcomer welcome. Bors was the only one to recognize Galahad as Lancelot's son. He took great glee and amusement in watching his fellow knights' warm reactions to the young stranger, especially that of the unknowing Lancelot.

The king later led Galahad to the river's edge, where the youngster succeeded in pulling the sword from the stone (see Seven of Swords). Having achieved both the Perilous Seat and the sword, the knights understood that the young and gentle man in their midst was destined to achieve the ultimate quest—the Quest for the Holy Grail.

QUEEN OF CUPS

MEANING

A woman with an Otherworldly air. She is creative with a wealth of artistic ability. A delicate, romantic beauty. A woman who is acutely sensitive
to her environment. One who trusts her intuitive sense and psychic abilities. A poetic person of vision and intelligence. A realistic woman of
strength and integrity. Can represent love and a happy marriage.

REVERSED

A dreamer and show-off. A shallow person with little conviction or honour. One who spouts nonsense and believes herself of superior intellect.
Dishonesty and immorality.

BRITANNIA

The early Celtic people believed that the spirit of the land was personified by the Goddess Sovereignty, who bore the same name as the land she represented.

The physical appearance of the Goddess often reflected the landscape and its current state. In the winter months she appeared as a dirty, weather-worn hag, with hair of lichen and arms and legs that resembled the bare limbs of trees. In the spring and summer she became a fertile, radiant beauty.

In many of the old tales, Sovereignty would first appear in her repulsive guise and test the would-be king. If she deemed him worthy of her, she would transform into her floral beauty of spring. The king's first duty was to the land, and upon taking the crown the king underwent a solemn ceremony in which he was bound in a sacred marriage to the land—a vow that the welfare of all depended upon. As the story of the Fisher King illustrates, if the king failed his responsibilities or was wounded, Sovereignty would transform to her loathly guise, the land would become barren, and all would suffer until the king was healed or replaced (most often the latter resolved the matter).

The Irish Sovereignty, Eriu (Ireland), appears in an early Irish story in which Conn of the Hundred Battles finds himself in the Otherworld court of Lug (which in many ways parallels the court of the Fisher King). Here, a young woman bore a golden cup and was called the Sovereignty of Ireland. In the stories, Peredur (approximately thirteenth-century Welsh) and Perlesvaus (thirteenth-century French) the Grail bearer appear as both the beautiful maid and repulsive crone. In light of this, it seems logical to assume that the figure who bears the Grail in the home of the Fisher King is the Sovereignty of Britain, sometimes called Brigit, Brigantia, or Britannia. Elaine, daughter of the Fisher King, is occasionally assigned the role of Grail bearer, and may have symbolically represented the goddess of the land.

Britain continues the tradition of having a female figure personify the land (or more recently, the British Empire). Today, she is embodied in the image of Britannia, who is depicted with a helmet, shield, and trident.

KING OF CUPS

MEANING

A mature, dignified man of authority. Someone who may be relied upon for guidance and assurance. A man of strong faith and liberal views. A person who displays an interest in the arts and sciences. One whose strength lies in his mind, which when combined with his uncanny foresight, is capable of orchestrating and achieving long-term goals. Can represent a lawyer, successful businessman, scientist, or artist. A person who tends to be reclusive and carries an air of mystery.

REVERSED

Dubious dealings. Loss and suffering. Illness and injustice. A man who lacks a sense of responsibility, and cares only for his personal welfare. Treachery and scandal.

THE FISHER KING

Fisher King was the name given to the succession of kings who were entrusted to guard the Grail; some of whom are Brons (or Helbron), Pelles, and Anfortas.

The goal of the Quest was to reach the elusive home of the Fisher King and ask the (correctly worded) question. It was believed that this would unlock the secret of the Grail, whereupon the king would be healed of his wound and the wasteland would rejuvenate. Here the Maimed King or Wounded King motif has fused with the already confounded nature of the Fisher King. Adding to the confusion is that there can be up to three wounded kings.

Brons is one of the first Fisher Kings, who in Robert de Borron's work suffers from (great) old age but has no wound. It is explained in Borron's *Joseph of Arimathea* that upon the command of God, Brons caught a fish and placed it with the Grail, where it became part of a mystic meal from which only the worthy could partake. Therefore, Brons is called "The Rich Fisher."

In the work of Chrétien de Troyes, there are two kings. One suffers from old age and is the father of the wounded Fisher King. Chrétien reasons that the King is called "Fisher" King because of his fondness for fishing. The *Parzival* of von Eschenbach is the same in having two kings, but here the old man is the grandfather. Lastly, when we turn to the *Queste* there are three kings: Pelles, his father, and Mordrain. Pelles and his father are both within the Grail Castle, and either one may be referred to as the Fisher King.

Percivale—and later, Galahad—were descendants of the Grail Guardians. In the case of Percivale, once he has achieved his Quest and land and king are whole, Percivale is appointed the "Keeper of the High Word," thus releasing his elders from their charge, allowing them to pass on to the Otherworld. In the tale of Galahad, the hero heals the king and his land, and then withdraws from this world with the Grail.

Some maintain that the Fisher King is a Christian motif, owing to the early Christian symbol of the fish; others argue that Brons is the avatar of the Welsh Bran the Blessed who suffered from a wounded foot. It is further explained that the fish equates with the Celtic Salmon of Knowledge (see Page of Cups). Continuing on the Celtic line, some consider Pelles to be the original Fisher King, and connect him with Pwyll of the Welsh *Mabinogion*.

It has been theorized that the wise Fisher King was the central figure of an age-old symbolic rejuvenation ritual that involved the phallic symbol of the spear and its feminine counterpart, the cup/cauldron. In this line of thought, the ritual healing of the king, who was bound in a sacred marriage to the land, was performed to bring renewal and fertility to the earth.

Though we may never know the origins of the Fisher/Maimed King, it would seem that most instinctively relate and intuitively feel the old magick that surrounds the figure. The magnetic Fisher King and his wasting lands continue to fascinate our modern world—perhaps with good reason (also see Queen of Cups).

SHIELDS

THE SUIT OF SHIELDS

Shields (Pentacles, Disks, Coins, etc.) represent the earthly material plane.

The shield is symbolic of security which brings stability and provides a foundation upon which one may build. As in the literal use of the shield, the suit represents a strength that protects and sustains through adversity.

The assets represented by the suit are not limited to material wealth, rather the cards may refer to a talent or skill that provides security. The suit of Shields reflects the aspects of mundane life which one values—money, property, career, etc.

Shields are symbolic of the material comfort levels of our physical existence. They can represent the fruits of one's labour, an inheritance, a new home, business transactions, craftsmanship, and improving one's skills.

The suit of Shields is associated with the earth and the season of winter.

ACE OF SHIELDS

ACE OF SHIELDS

EVALACH'S SHIELD

MEANING

Treasures. Prosperity. Making great gains. Receiving a wealth of recognition for achievements. An unexpected inheritance. A lucrative business venture. Ecstasy and gratitude. Freedom and confidence. Enjoying the beauty of nature. Enriching the spirit. The combination of material and emotional well-being. Attainment and contentment.

REVERSED

Greed. Corruption. Basing one's self-worth on material commodities. Wasting resources. Material wealth without self-satisfaction. Believing money to be success. Hoarding. Refusing to share with others.

EVALACH'S SHIELD

The monks reveal the mysterious shield of centuries past.

In the Grail romances, Evalach the Unknown was the heathen King of Sarras. He was befriended by Joseph of Arimathea who found Evalach enthroned in a rich sun temple within the city of Sarras. Joseph eventually managed to convert Evalach to the Christian faith, though judging by his baptismal name, Mordrain ("slow of belief"), one might guess that this was not an easy task.

Joseph gave his friend a shield of miraculous powers, which depicted the scene of the crucifixion. Evalach carried the shield into battle with Tholomer. The sight unnerved his opponents and brought victory to Evalach. After the battle, the shield performed a second miracle by restoring a soldier's severed hand; the scene on the shield then faded, never to return.

Joseph of Arimathea made his way to Britain, reputedly bringing with him the Grail, or chalice of the Last Supper. Evalach followed, bringing the treasured shield into the future land of Arthur. Legend claims that the Holy Grail first came to rest in Avalon (Glastonbury). It was during this time that Evalach approached too near the Grail and was struck down. His dare left him a blind invalid, destined to languish in this world for hundreds of years, until Galahad released him. While upon his deathbed Joseph thought to leave his earthbound friend something to remember him by, and stained Evalach's shield with a cross of his own blood.

Evalach established an abbey and placed the shield in its care. Over the years rumours circulated, attracting knights who tried and failed to bear the shield. None could ride more than a few miles from the abbey without being assaulted by a white phantom knight who insisted the shield be returned. Thus, when Galahad arrived at the abbey, the shield of Evalach awaited him. On leaving the abbey, Galahad met the white knight, only this time the phantom relayed the history of the shield and then vanished.

It is believed that Evalach of these tales originates from the Welsh god Avallach (which may be spelled numerous ways). Not much is known of Avallach, beyond being the son of the god Beli or Belinus and father of Modron, also known as the Goddess Matrona, attributes of which Morgan partly embodies. According to William of Malmesbury, Avalloc chose to live with his daughters near Glastonbury, or Avalon, due to the privacy of the area. When we consider the names of Avallach (apple orchard) and the Isle of Avalon or "Ynys Avallach," as it appears in Welsh, one can see why Avallach is sometimes called the King of Avalon. It is worth remembering that Avalon of Glastonbury was not the only Otherworld Isle of Apples (apples being sacred to the early Celts), and so the question as to the domain of Avallach, and from where his name derives, remains unanswered.

TWO OF SHIELDS

MEANING

The successful handling of fluctuating fortune. Having to adjust to unforeseen difficulties. Encountering obstacles which press for a re-evaluation of plans. Trying to launch a project with a limited amount of funds. Recognizing the humour in minor mishaps that would otherwise cause embarrassment. Reassessment calls for creative manoeuvres to avert troubled waters.

REVERSED

Dismissing indications of trouble. Lack of attention to details. Poor planning leads to humiliation. Disharmony among teammates. An erratic phase. Inability to adapt and meet new challenges.

CASTLE PENDRAGON

Uther looks upon puddles where he had planned a moat. According to folklore, when Uther built his Castle Pendragon, he envisioned grand fortifications, the most spectacular of which was to be the moat.

Uther planned to divert the River Eden to surround the castle, thus forming an effective moat. Though this project was impressive in theory the River Eden held many surprises and refused to cooperate, forcing the frustrated king and his weary workmen to abandon the effort. Hence the saying—Let Uther Pendragon do what he can, Eden will run where Eden ran.

By the time of Arthur's reign, Castle Pendragon had fallen into the hands of Sir Brian de les Isles. Despite the efforts made to win his loyalty, Brian de les Isles refused to swear allegiance to Arthur.

On returning from the Adventure of the Black Shield (see Four of Spears), Lancelot and La Cote Male Tail passed by Castle Pendragon, where they encountered the rebel knight. As a result of his confrontation with Lancelot, Brian was put off his lands and lost the castle. Following his banishment, Lancelot gave the castle and its surrounding lands to the young La Cote Male Tail and his bride to be.

THREE OF SHIELDS

THREE OF SHIELDS

THE HOMESPUN
TUNIC

MEANING

Skill and growth. Making progress in one's vocation. Meaningful, constructive use of talents. Pursuing a dream with the advice and cooperation of others. Laying a foundation and gathering the material goods needed for future exploits. An increasing sense of identity and purpose. The card indicates the success of ventures being planned at this time.

REVERSED

Doubting the path one has chosen. Lack of enthusiasm and self-confidence. Not realizing one's potential. Wasting talent. Poor quality work. Dismissing sound advice.

THE HOMESPUN TUNIC

Percivale's mother consoles herself by making a new tunic for her beloved son.

Having led a sheltered life, the young Percivale believed he was seeing angels when he encountered knights travelling through the forest. After the seemingly divine creatures had passed, Percivale ran home to his mother, who in turn explained that the angels were in reality knights. The widow looked on helplessly as her greatest fear came to pass—her son now longed to be a knight. Percivale would not be deterred; he had found his calling and planned to seek out the king they called Arthur, maker of knights. In watching Percivale's eyes dance, his mother knew all her efforts to shield him had been futile, and resigned herself to do all she could to prepare him for what lay ahead. For the first time she told her son of his noble blood and of the many honourable knights of the family, all of whom had met with misfortune. She herself was of a great family, one for which there had been no equal. Tragedy struck, however, leaving her to raise her son in an impoverished state. In a warm voice, she kindly explained that in being of such noble blood, Arthur would not deny him his knighthood, but warned that he had much to learn of the life of arms. First and foremost, she counselled her son to always honour ladies and never deny them aid, for if he did, he would be a knight without worship.

As Percivale prepared for his journey, the grieving mother found comfort in making a new tunic for her son. It was a large tunic of the Welsh fashion; something to remind Percivale of his home in future times of high adventure. When the day of his departure arrived, Percivale's mother gave him the cherished tunic, which he would wear next to his skin for many a year.

Donning his new garment and high spirits, Percivale then left his mother and made his way to Arthur's court.

FOUR OF SHIELDS

MEANING

Financial stability. Expansion. Building and development. Opening one's doors to business. Commercial endeavour. Spending money on luxury items. Basing one's identity on material possessions. Hunger for power and influence. An ostentatious show of wealth. Trying to buy the respect of others. Acquiring possessions. A love of money. Seeking prestige.

REVERSED

Modest ambition. A reluctance to risk. Playing it safe. Overburdening one's self with responsibilities. A need to be in control of all aspects of a project breeds resentment in the workplace. A reversal of fortune.

KING MARK

King Mark's increasingly extravagant plans for his banquet hall exasperate his clerk.

According to legend, King Mark of Cornwall was Tristram's uncle, and Isolt of Ireland's husband. Though most say the relationship between Mark and his nephew began favourably, a deadly rivalry brewed once Isolt and the king were married.

At times Mark is portrayed as an understanding man, who while being sympathetic to the fated love of Tristram and Isolt, could not abide the humiliation. Other times he appears as a selfish man with no honour who is responsible for his nephew's murder. Mark has also been depicted in a comedic light. Possibly due to some confusion surrounding his name, Mark (the Welsh "March," meaning "horse"), the king has been depicted with horse ears. Like the donkey-eared Midas of Greek legend, Mark acquired a greedy, shallow reputation.

The earthwork fort known as Castle Dore, in Cornwall, is considered to have been the home of the sixth-century King Cynvawr, who some equate with King Mark, though this has yet to be proven. Excavations at the site have revealed that it was reoccupied during the fifth century. At this time, the largest structure on the site was a hall of considerable size, measuring 90 by 40 feet, and judging by the size of its post holes, it was, in its day, a grand building.

FIVE OF SHIELDS

MEANING

The exhaustion of resources. Lack of money and energy. Struggling to stay afloat. Undergoing a desolate phase in life. Being faced with a barren landscape. Fighting to keep one's spirits up. Feeling abandoned. Having to adapt to a change of fortune. Yearning for guidance. Moving on in search of nourishment. Temporary hardships. Poverty.

REVERSED

Creating troubles. Continuing on a destructive path. Not recognizing when one ought to retreat in order to cut losses. Wasting money. Indulging in excesses.

THE WASTELAND

The destitute inhabitants travel their wasting lands.

The Wasteland is the name given to the barren country that surrounds the Grail Castle. Due to the sacred bond between land and king, the once lush and fertile realm suffers as a consequence of the wound inflicted upon her king (see Ace of Spears).

In her wasting state, the land is stripped of her vegetation; she bears no animals nor crops. Her rivers run dry and her childless inhabitants live in grief and fear.

The concept of the Wasteland is thought to be of Celtic origin, and is not limited to being the result of a wounded king. The suffering land can reflect the king's overall inadequacy to rule. In the sacred marriage of king to land, he swears to serve her before all else. If the king should ever forsake his vow, whether it be by abusing his power, neglect, or through making poor choices, the land was destined to waste and the people to suffer. At times the Wasteland is said to mirror the illness or extreme old age of the king. Other times it is said to be the result of the knight's failure to ask the appropriate questions. And in some instances it is the effect of prolonged war, or the death of a much-loved knight upon whom the land depends.

Only when the Quest is achieved—when the hero asks the appropriate questions and restores the king—shall the land be free of the curse which rests upon her.

SIX OF SHIELDS

MEANING

Generosity and kindness. Receiving help from others. A sense of relief as a burden is lifted from one's shoulders. An improvement in circumstances. Receiving a gift. Material gain. Sympathetic and supportive friends. Charitable acts. Sharing one's knowledge and experience. Sharing good fortune. A windfall. Gratitude. Lucrative business transactions.

REVERSED

Accumulating debts. Mishandling financial matters. Investing in dubious money-making schemes. Underhanded dealings. Theft and greed. Jealousy and exploitation. Future plans delayed by outstanding debts.

CASTLE OF MAIDENS

Galahad restores the castle to its rightful heiress.

During his Quest, Galahad came upon a deserted chapel upon a mountain. As he knelt to pray before its altar he heard a voice that commanded him to seek out the Castle of Maidens and do away with its wicked custom. Galahad did as he was instructed and found the castle beside the River Severn. As he approached the stronghold an old man warned him not to venture any further, as the castle was occupied by seven murderous knights who kept many women captive for their private pleasures. There then came seven maids, and after that, a squire, all of whom repeated the warning. Knowing this to be his charge, Galahad disregarded their pleas and pressed on.

The seven knights emerged from their lair to confront the stranger, demanding that he ride on or face his death. Galahad challenged and overcame all seven knights, who on losing their courage ran to the forest for cover.

The wronged women of the castle then appeared and thanked their champion. Fearing the return of the villains, the chief lady suggested that Galahad summon all the people of the surrounding lands and have them swear to return to the old ways. Galahad agreed and blew an ivory horn, calling all locals to the castle. As he awaited their arrival, Galahad was told how seven years previously, the seven knights had slain the lord of the castle and taken his daughters (and many maids since) hostage. After three days of enduring the evils of the knights the elder daughter died, but fortunately the younger daughter survived. On learning this, Galahad made all of the local residents pay homage to the daughter as the rightful heir of the castle and its lands.

The following day Galahad received word that the seven knights had encountered Gawain and his brothers in the forest. In the battle that followed, all seven evil knights had met their death. Since all fears were now put to rest, Galahad returned to his Quest, leaving the Castle of Maidens and its lands under the rule of the women.

SEVEN OF SHIELDS

MEANING

Treasures. Bounty. Ingenuity and perseverance bring great gains. Success-fully handling a challenging and complex situation. Patience and restraint prove to be appropriate. The steady, methodical removal of obstacles. Concentrating and completing one task at a time allows for safe progress to greater heights.

REVERSED

Impatience. Unfulfilled hopes of promotion. Worrying delays. Stiff com-petition. Unexpected setbacks. Confusion as to how one should best pro-ceed. Miscalculation. Unease in regard to financial matters.

CASTLE OF WONDERS

The greatest treasure of the castle was its miraculous pillar, which brought the entire kingdom to life within its column.

Like the Castle of Maidens, the Castle of Wonders held many women captive within its walls. The castle and its 500 residents were bound by a powerful spell, cast by the Otherworldly magician Klingsor.

Determined to release the women, Gawain entered the enchanted castle. Within its ornate hall stood an equally beautiful bed. Gawain approached the bed, but as he tried to sit upon it, it moved of its own accord. The knight accepted the challenge, threw himself upon it, and held on with all his might. The possessed bed hurled itself about the room, slamming into walls with tremendous force. As it came to rest, the shaken knight was subjected to a second ordeal. An ungodly rain of stones pelted down upon him, nearly knocking him senseless. This was followed by a deadly rain of arrows fired by a mechanized army of archers who were affixed to the walls of the hall. The bewildered Gawain could hardly believe what he saw, and found it harder still to believe he had survived. Lastly, the battered knight faced an enormous lion which burst into the hall. Gawain threw himself into battle with the giant cat, and in mustering all his strength overcame the beast. In doing so, he broke the enchantment that lay over the castle.

Eager to show their gratitude, the women of the castle led Gawain to the chamber which held the castle's treasures, the finest of which was a magnificent pillar. The magical pillar was like no other; one could view the entire kingdom within the column. Every creature, movement, stone, and stream could be seen upon its living surface.

It was explained to Gawain that the kingdom, castle, and its miraculous pillar could all be his if he agreed to stay with the women he had freed. Gawain was honoured and grateful for the offer, but on careful consideration decided that his heart lay with his life as a Knight of the Round Table, to which he then returned.

EIGHT OF SHIELDS

MEANING

Employment. Commissions. Craftsmanship. The positive, productive use of one's skills. Focusing one's energy on work. Employment that brings self-satisfaction. Intense labour. A creative endeavour. Learning a new skill or trade. Having a modest attitude toward accomplishments. Enjoying work and the rewards it brings.

REVERSED

Dreading the workplace. Feeling trapped, unmotivated, and despondent. Disappointment. An unfulfilling profession. Producing poor quality work. Exploitation, vanity, and hypocrisy.

WAYLAND

Deep within the earth, Wayland practices his craft.

The Saxon smith Wayland is the Norse smith Völundr who became incorporated into the mythology of Britain. Wayland was the master craftsman to the gods, whose weapons were so fine that they sang in the air. Excalibur is sometimes said to have been forged by Wayland. The coveted work of this god of smiths led King Nidud to abduct him. Nidud hamstrung the smith to prevent his escape and then forced his lame prisoner to work. The art of the smith and magician were thought to be closely related, and it was by magic that the smith eventually escaped the clutches of Nidud, after which he sought a terrible revenge upon the king's family.

Over time, Wayland has come to be associated with many of Britain's ancient sites, and appears in Geoffrey of Monmouth's *The Life of Merlin*. The spirit of Wayland is said to haunt a neolithic burial chamber known as Wayland's Smithy in Oxfordshire. Tradition maintains that if one were to leave a horse and coin at the chamber overnight, on returning in the morning one would find the coin gone and the horse shod.

NINE OF SHIELDS

MEANING

Prudence and discretion. Foresight brings success. Adhering to one's values. Discernment and personal honour. Accomplishment by way of goodwill toward others. Diplomacy and patience. Following through on plans. Honouring a promise. Fulfilling obligations. Popularity. Receiving and enjoying rewards.

REVERSED

Shallow, spiteful behaviour. Broken promises. A weak character. Ignoring old friends. Not acknowledging the assistance of others. A social climber. A superficial person who humiliates others to boost his or her own self-confidence.

RAGNELL

As her despondent husband gazes into the fire, the Loathly Lady sheds her skin and emerges as the comely Ragnell.

Arthur entered an enchanted land that drained all the courage from his heart and strength from his limbs. The ruler of the kingdom thought to play with his prey and agreed to release Arthur from the spell for one year. Within that year Arthur must find the answer to the riddle "What does a woman want most?" If he should fail, he would be condemned to live out his days as a prisoner of the enchanted land.

As the king returned to his court he passed through a forest, where he came across a hideous old woman seated between a holly tree and an oak. The lady wore a dress of scarlet, but despite its full fabric one could see her deformed figure beneath. Her filthy skin was the colour of bark, and her arms and legs were knotted and twisted like the limbs of a weatherworn tree. One eye was black, the other a milky yellow. Her gaping mouth and misshapen nose slid to one side of her face, and her hair had the look of lichen. But despite her appearance the woman was well-spoken and offered to help the king answer the riddle, provided he grant her whatever she wished. Arthur was stunned by this sight, but agreed. On hearing her request, the king again found himself in an impossible situation—the Loathly Lady wished the handsome Gawain to be her husband. Refusing to ask such a thing of his nephew, the king left the crone and returned to the court.

Word of Arthur's predicament reached Gawain, who thinking to save his king and help the woman, searched the forest. Having found the crone, Gawain assured her that if any of the court dared ridicule her they would regret it. At Gawain's coaxing, the lady came to the court where they were wed before a bewildered crowd. Despite the sneering and excitement, Gawain never left her side and remained courteous throughout the evening.

After retiring to their bedchamber Gawain's heart began to wane. He stared into the fire, desperately trying to think how he might avoid the bed without insulting his bride. When he turned to face her, he found not the hideous crone, but a beautiful woman in her place. Ragnell explained to her husband that she was the same woman he had wed earlier that day, and that now he faced a difficult decision—he must choose whether he wished his wife hideous by day and beautiful by night, or beautiful by day and hideous by night. Gawain thought over the question Ragnell had posed, and replied that the choice must be hers, adding that he would be content whatever her decision. At once a smile came across Ragnell's face, who then told Gawain that given his response she would now remain his loving and beautiful wife both day and night, for he had answered the enchanter's riddle: "What does a woman desire most?"—Her own way.

TEN OF SHIELDS

MEANING

Wealth and prosperity. Enjoying home and family. Sharing good fortune with one's kin. Maintaining a family tradition. Benefiting from security and prominence established by predecessors. Inheritance. Affluence and riches. Enjoying the rewards and celebrations that follow the completion of a mission. Clan gatherings. Participating in traditions.

REVERSED

Domestic strife resulting from financial worries. Material loss. Gambling and theft. Having to live under a tight budget. Restriction and possible loss of inheritance.

CAMELOT

With the arrival of winter, halls fill and hearts lift.

Chrétien de Troyes names Arthur's court Camelot in his medieval romance *Lancelot*. Over the centuries the vision of Camelot has most often been based on the medieval, romantic ideal rather than the Dark Age reality.

Merlin was the architect of the fabled Camelot. Some claimed that the magician completed the castle in a single night. Within its great walls stood the Round Table and its noble Fellowship, dreams of which seduced many would-be knights to seek its ivory towers. Being the High King, Arthur was forced to hold court throughout his realm, but Camelot remained his seat of power and favoured home.

There are a number of contenders for the site of Arthur's court, including Caerleon, Winchester, and Colchester. An Iron Age hill fort near the village of South Cadbury in Somerset has become the favoured site of many. Excavations at Cadbury have revealed that it was reoccupied and its defenses strengthened during the time of Arthur's reputed rule.

The Dark Age court may not have been as fanciful as the medieval ideal, but if we are to judge by the insights that early poems provide, we may well say it was at least comfortable. Summer was the active season of campaigning (or raiding), while winter was the time when the king and his warband reaped their rewards and returned to the warmth of hearth and home. In order to secure his standing and the loyalty of his followers, the chieftain would play the generous host throughout the winter. His hall would be furnished with couches and tables, enough to accommodate all. Jesters, games, and music entertained the guests, while meats roasted over central hearths. Wine, mead, and ale were served, but were not considered an excuse for bad manners, particularly in the company of women. The firelit halls nurtured laughter, romance, and all-important alliances. For the people of the Dark Ages these were times to feast, love, and aspire to the heroic tales and songs of the resident bards. Above all, these dark nights were to be enjoyed!

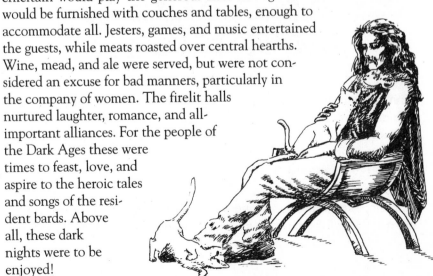

PAGE OF SHIELDS

MEANING

A tenacious, reliable person. One who resists any distractions when in pursuit of a goal. A serious scholar with great self-discipline. A hunger for knowledge. A dedicated student. One who exhibits a keen business sense. An honourable, courageous person who does his or her best to help others. A messenger bringing good news.

REVERSED

A meticulous worker, but one who lacks compassion or a sense of humour. One who has difficulty relating to others and resents those who do. A lack of imagination. Wastefulness. Unwelcome news.

THE BADGER

In folklore, the badger has come to symbolize strength and courage—the two qualities that have earned the animal much respect. The badger retains its early formidable reputation in more recent works such as Kenneth Grahame's *The Wind in the Willows*. Here, the badger is the established authority and the respected resident of the Wild Wood whom the other creatures depend upon for guidance, strength, and protection.

To encounter a badger before a battle would be considered a favourable omen, portending bravery and endurance. The badger represents resisting panic, surmounting one's fears, and guarding that which one holds dear.

KNIGHT OF SHIELDS

MEANING

An honest, hard-working man. A supporter of tradition and order. A polite, capable man who is genuinely committed to achieving his full potential. An ambitious yet compassionate man. A responsible, loyal companion who offers practical advice. Solid, steadfast progress. A dependable young man. Patience, perseverance, and stamina.

REVERSED

Lack of direction. Intolerance and narrow-mindedness. Stagnation and complacency. A bully who holds himself in high regard. Intimidation. One who seeks to sustain power by oppressing the ideas and dreams of others.

BORS

Bors was Lancelot's cousin and one of Arthur's best knights. Throughout his life, Bors remained a steadfast supporter of his king. Perhaps the best known trial endured by Bors was the impossible decision he faced of either helping a young woman or his brother, both of whom were in immediate danger. As Bors approached a crossroads he saw a maid being carried off by a lecherous knight in one direction, and in the opposite direction he could see two knights who beat upon his brother Lionel. Bors chose to save the maid, and in the time it took him to return, Lionel had managed to overcome his enemies. Thinking his brother had forsaken him, Lionel was blind with rage and lunged at Bors. A desperate battle began; their tempers became so hot that the struggle may have been fatal. As Bors made ready to strike his deadly blow a brilliant raging wall of flame burst forth, separating the two men. The miraculous sight caused the brothers to retreat and drop their weapons. The flames succeeded in ending the battle and preventing tragedy, though from that day forward the brothers did not speak to one another.

By some accounts, Bors was a model knight, second only to Galahad. In being totally dedicated to his Quest, Bors had intended to remain chaste throughout his days. Yet during his adventures and trials he was magically seduced by the daughter of King Brangorre, who then gave birth to Helain le Blanc. Nevertheless, this incident did not prevent him from accompanying Galahad and Percivale to the Grail Castle and achieving the Quest.

THE QUEEN OF SHIELDS

MEANING

A sensible, considerate person. A woman of influence who uses her power to help those less fortunate. One with a stately air about her who gives generously of herself. She has a strong sense for business and is an effective advocate. A dignified woman with an inherent sense of responsibility. She can indicate wealth, security, and independence.

REVERSED

Suspicion and fear. Sensing a threat to one's security. Not feeling comfortable with having to rely on others. An unhealthy preoccupation with money. Disorientation and worry. Unscrupulous behaviour.

IGRAINE

Igraine was the graceful wife of Gorlois, the Duke of Cornwall. She was much loved by her husband who was a loyal supporter of Uther Pendragon. The king valued their friendship, as Gorlois was mature in years and his knowledge and experience were great assets upon the battlefield. However, their relationship turned sour when Gorlois brought his fair young wife to London and introduced her to the king. Uther fell in love with her at first sight and gave her all of his attention. He did his utmost to engage her in conversation, sent the finest foods to her table, and ordered his personal attendants to serve her. Flattered though she was, Igraine was a married woman and began to feel uncomfortable under Uther's gaze. The king's infatuation had not gone unnoticed by the duke, who then returned Igraine to Tintagel Castle. This action prompted a battle between the duke and king (see Five of Spears).

Uther managed to reach his love by the craft of Merlin, who changed him into the likeness of the duke, which allowed him to freely enter the castle; Arthur was conceived that night.

Some say that Igraine received Uther, believing him to be her husband. Others say his disguise was for the benefit of the guards alone and that Igraine secretly harboured and equalled Uther's passion. Whether Igraine loved him at this time or not, she did come to love him, and it was a great and passionate love which lasted all of their days. After the death of Gorlois, Uther married Igraine, mother of his son Arthur. Theirs was a happy marriage; the people loved their High Queen and henceforth Igraine ruled alongside her husband as an equal partner.

KING OF SHIELDS

MEANING

An authority figure who possesses great leadership abilities. A decisive, courageous man. A loyal, supportive husband. A distinguished man of strong character. An admired businessman. Security. Protection. Sound investments. Profitable business manoeuvres. Expansion and progress.

REVERSED

Dishonourable behaviour. Corruption. A sneaky, unscrupulous opponent. Employee unrest. Divided loyalties. A cantankerous old man. Taking unwise financial risks.

UTHER

Uther Pendragon was the younger brother of Ambrosius and father of Arthur. At the time of Ambrosius' death a dragon-shaped comet passed over Britain. All expected Uther to succeed his brother, and now Merlin explained that the comet was a favourable omen of Uther's coming reign, and the reign of his yet unborn son. The appearance of the comet led Uther to assume the name "Pendragon," meaning "Head Dragon." Once Uther had been crowned, he continued his advance on the invading Saxons and was most often successful. Over time, this hard life took its toll on the king and he became ill. Too weakened to continue on the battlefield, Uther appointed a wise and experienced friend to direct his forces. However, the chain of command began to break down without Uther's strong leadership. The British leaders quarrelled amongst themselves and were no longer capable of putting up a unified front. In Uther's absence the Britons were overcome by the Saxon force, who then laid waste to the land. The Saxon leader Octa, whom Uther had previously captured, escaped from his prison and fled to Germany. There he raised an army of reinforcements and returned to renew his invasion of Britain.

Uther was furious with the British leaders and demanded a litter be built in which he could be carried on to the battlefield. Hence Uther led his men again. On hearing that their great adversary was reduced to being borne in a litter, the Saxons refused to fight, believing it was beneath them. Though they no longer feared Uther the great warrior, Uther the great leader remained a powerful enemy. Uther provoked the Saxons into battle and gave them cause to regret their confidence. Octa was killed in battle and again the Saxons were driven back.

Knowing that if they were to make progress they would have to kill Uther, the Saxons sent spies to monitor the king's health. Though the king was very near death, he would occasionally make slight improvements. This worried the Saxon's leaders, who ordered the spies to poison the spring from which Uther drank. The king died immediately, leaving his wife Igraine and his young son to contend with the Saxons, who became bolder upon the king's death.

BIBLIOGRAPHY

Alcock, Leslie. *Arthur's Britain*. Penguin Books, 1990.

Ashe, Geoffrey. *Mythology of the British Isles*. London: Methuen, 1990.

Ashe, Geoffrey, ed. *The Quest for Arthur's Britain*. Paladin Books, 1986.

Atkinson, R. J. C. *Stonehenge and Neighbouring Monuments*. London: Historic Buildings and Monuments Commission for England, 1985.

Barber, Richard, ed. *The Arthurian Legends*. Barnes & Noble Books, 1993.

Bellingham, David. *An Introduction to Celtic Mythology*. Quintet Publishing Limited, 1990.

Bord, Janet and Colin. *Mysterious Britain*. Paladin Books, 1989.

Bunney, Sarah, ed. *The Illustrated Book of Herbs*. Octopus Books Limited, 1984.

Burl, Aubrey. *Prehistoric Avebury*. Yale University Press, 1979.

Chant, Joy. *The High Kings*. Bantam Books, 1983.

Chetwynd, Tom. *Dictionary of Symbols*. Aquarian Press, 1993.

Chrétien de Troyes. *The Complete Romances of Chrétien de Troyes*. Trans. with introduction by David Staines. Indiana University Press, 1990.

Churchill, Winston S. *The Island Race*. New York: Dodd, Mead and Company, 1964.

Clayton, Peter. *Great Figures of Mythology*. Bison Books Limited, 1990.

Conway, D. J. *Celtic Magic*. Llewellyn Publications, 1990.

Douglas, Alfred. *The Tarot*. Arkana Penguin Books Limited, 1991.

Ebbutt, M.I. *The British*. (Myths and Legends Series.) London: Bracken Books, 1985.

Ellis, Peter Berresford. *Dictionary of Celtic Mythology*. Constable, 1992.

Frazer, J. G. *The Golden Bough*. (Abridged edition.) Papermac, 1987.

Geoffrey of Monmouth. *The History of the Kings of Britain*. Trans. with introduction by Lewis Thorpe. Penguin Books, 1966.

Greer, Mary K. *Tarot for Yourself*. Newcastle Publishing Company, 1984.

Hall, Calvin S., and Vernon J. Nordby. *A Primer of Jungian Psychology*. Mentor Books, 1973.

Hebbert, Antonia, ed. *Secret Britain*. UK: Automobile Association, 1986.

Jayanti, Amber. *Living the Tarot*. Llewellyn Publications, 1993.

Jung, Carl, ed. *Man and his Symbols*. Laurel Books, 1968.

Junjulas, Craig. *Psychic Tarot*. Morgan and Morgan Inc. Publishers, 1985.

Kaplan, Stuart R. *The Encyclopedia of the Tarot: Volume I*. U.S. Games Systems Inc., 1978.

Kaplan, Stuart R. *The Encyclopedia of the Tarot: Volume II*. U.S. Games Systems Inc., 1986.

King, Francis X. *The Encyclopedia of Fortune-Telling*. Gallery Books, 1988.

Knight, Gareth. *Tarot and Magic*. Destiny Books, 1991.

Lacy, Norris J., ed. *The Arthurian Encyclopedia*. Peter Bedrick Books, 1986.

Laing, Lloyd. *Celtic Britain*. Charles Scribner's Sons, 1979.

Lee, Allan. text by David Day, *Castles*. Bantam Books, 1984.

Lehane, Brendan. *Legends of Valour*. (The Enchanted World series.) Time-Life Books, 1984.

Lehane, Brendan. *Wizards and Witches*. (The Enchanted World series.) Time-Life Books, 1984.

Loomis, Roger Sherman. *Celtic Myth and Arthurian Romance*. Columbia University Press, 1927.

Loomis, Roger Sherman. *The Grail from Celtic Myth to Christian Symbol*. Constable and Company Limited, 1992.

Loomis, Roger Sherman. *Wales and the Arthurian Legend*. Cardiff: University of Wales Press, 1956.

Mabinogion. Trans. with introduction by Gwyn and Thomas Jones. Dragon's Dream Books, 1982.

Malory, Sir Thomas. *Le Morte d'Arthur*. Caxton's text, with introduction by John Rhys. Toronto: B. Mitchell, 1985.

Matthews, Caitlin and John. *An Encyclopedia of Myth and Legend, British and Irish Mythology*. Aquarian Press, 1988.

Matthews, John, ed. *An Arthurian Reader*. Aquarian Press, 1988.

Minary, Ruth and Charles Moorman. *An Arthurian Dictionary*. Academy Chicago Publishers, 1990.

Phillips, Ellen. *The Fall of Camelot*. (The Enchanted World series.) Time-Life Books, 1986.

Phillips, Ellen. *Seekers and Saviors*. (The Enchanted World series.) Time-Life Books, 1986.

Pollack, Rachel. *Seventy-Eight Degrees of Wisdom*. Aquarian Press, 1980.

Queste del Saint Graal. Trans. with introduction by P. M. Matarasso, *The Quest for the Holy Grail*. Penguin Books, 1969.

Rolleston, T. W. *Celtic Myths and Legends*. Bracken Books, London, 1985.

Rutherford, Ward. *Celtic Lore*. Aquarian/Thorsons, 1993.

Sir Gawain and the Green Knight. Trans. with introduction by Brian Stone. Penguin Books, 1974.

Stein, W. *A Colouring Book of Ancient Ireland*. Bellerophon Books, 1978.

Stewart, R. J. *Celtic Gods, Celtic Goddesses*. Blandford, 1990.

Tolstoy, Nikolai. *The Quest for Merlin*. Sceptre, 1988.

Weston, Jessie L. *From Ritual to Romance*. Cambridge University Press, 1920; Gloucester, MA: Peter Smith, 1983.

INDEX

☽ LOOK FOR THE CRESCENT MOON

Llewellyn publishes hundreds of books on your favorite subjects! To get these exciting books, including the ones on the following pages, check your local bookstore or order them directly from Llewellyn.

ORDER BY PHONE
- Call toll-free within the U.S. and Canada, 1-800-THE MOON
- In Minnesota, call (612) 291-1970
- We accept VISA, MasterCard, and American Express

ORDER BY MAIL
- Send the full price of your order (MN residents add 7% sales tax) in U.S. funds, plus postage & handling to:

  Llewellyn Worldwide
  P.O. Box 64383, Dept. K266-6
  St. Paul, MN 55164–0383, U.S.A.

POSTAGE & HANDLING
(For the U.S., Canada, and Mexico)
- $4.00 for orders $15.00 and under
- $5.00 for orders over $15.00
- No charge for orders over $100.00

We ship UPS in the continental United States. We ship standard mail to P.O. boxes. Orders shipped to Alaska, Hawaii, The Virgin Islands, and Puerto Rico are sent first-class mail. Orders shipped to Canada and Mexico are sent surface mail.

International orders: Airmail—add freight equal to price of each book to the total price of order, plus $5.00 for each non-book item (audio tapes, etc.).

Surface mail—Add $1.00 per item.

Allow 4–6 weeks for delivery on all orders.
Postage and handling rates subject to change.

DISCOUNTS
We offer a 20% discount to group leaders or agents. You must order a minimum of 5 copies of the same book to get our special quantity price.

FREE CATALOG
Get a free copy of our color catalog, *New Worlds of Mind and Spirit*. Subscribe for just $10.00 in the United States and Canada ($30.00 overseas, airmail). Many bookstores carry *New Worlds*—ask for it!

Visit our web site at www.llewellyn.com for more information.

ROBIN WOOD TAROT DECK
Created and illustrated by Robin Wood
Instructions by Robin Wood
and Michael Short

Tap into the wisdom of your subconscious with one of the most beautiful Tarot decks on the market today! Reminiscent of the Rider-Waite deck, the Robin Wood Tarot is flavored with nature imagery and luminous energies that will enchant you and the querant. Even the novice reader will find these cards easy and enjoyable to interpret.

Radiant and rich, these cards were illustrated with a unique technique that brings out the resplendent color of the prismacolor pencils. The shining strength of this Tarot deck lies in its depiction of the Minor Arcana. Unlike other Minor Arcana decks, this one springs to pulsating life. The cards are printed in quality card stock and boxed complete with instruction booklet, which provides the upright and reversed meanings of each card, as well as three basic card layouts. Beautiful and brilliant, the Robin Wood Tarot is a must-have deck!

0-87542-894-0, boxed set: 78-cards with booklet   **$19.95**

To order, call 1-800-THE MOON
All prices subject to change without notice

THE RUNE ORACLE

Cards created and illustrated
by Nigel Jackson
Rune Mysteries by Nigel Jackson and
Silver RavenWolf

The snow-covered peaks, misty heaths, dark woods and storm-wracked seas of the Northern World were the cradle of a remarkable and bold mysticism, whose essence is concentrated in the runes. The runes are a method of communicating with divinity—the god/goddess within each of us who embodies our pure consciousness and inward spirituality.

The Rune Oracle cards are rich in beautiful imagery; along with the accompanying book *Rune Mysteries*, they are a shortcut to the esoteric rune system. Here, old American witchcraft and European practices meld into a contemporary evolution of the Northern magickal lore. This system is of immediate and practical use in divination, magick, and self-development. Even a little experience at casting the Rune Oracle cards will soon convince you of the uncanny accuracy of their messages.

The card's images were subtly constructed to contain symbolic significance at a number of levels. This visual "unfolding" of each rune's inner mysteries within each card enables you to hear their oracular voices with greater clarity than was ever before possible except at the most advanced degrees of runic knowledge.

1-56718-364-6, Boxed set:
Book: *Rune Oracle*, 6 x 9, 256 pp., illus., softcover
Deck: 25 full-color cards $29.95

AWARENESS CARDS
Susan Halliday

The Awareness Cards are a powerful companion on the journey of self-discovery. Designed for today's seeker, this playful tarot deck features 48 full-color cards that blend primitive images with Jungian archetypes (i.e., Wild Woman, The Warrior, Petty Tyrants). The life-affirming meanings of the cards are found in the 288-page companion book.

Soft, whimsical, and personal, the cards speak immediately to people of all ages and cultures. The archetypes appeal to our modern roles in life, yet the pictures are essentially stylized petroglyphs—or adaptations of prehistoric carvings—from Celtic, Egyptian, Norse, Native American, as well as European paleolithic and mesolithic sources. A brief description of where these are (or were) located is found in the back of the book.

The book also includes five card spreads (Signal Spread, Energy Spread, Star Spread, Dream Spread, and Healing Spread) to help you understand the energy around you, gain insight into your current and developing relationships, and embark on the road to healing. Charts in the book show the astrological and numerological significance of the cards.

1-56718-344-1, Boxed set:
Book: 5⅜ x 6¼, 288 pp., illus., softcover
Deck: 48 full-color cards $19.95

To order, call 1-800-THE MOON
All prices subject to change without notice